Praise for *Engage to Win*

"To be successful in the Engagement Economy, today's marketer must understand the new digital landscape. This means engaging with today's buyers and prospects with relevance in every interaction with your brand. In *Engage to Win*, Steve Lucas introduces a brilliant three-step process for modern engagement—Listen, Learn, and Engage. *Engage to Win* is a must-read for companies looking to succeed."

—Stephen Yeo, Director of Marketing, Panasonic Europe

"Urgent, actionable insights from the front lines of our revolution. Marketing is never going to be the same, and Steve Lucas wants to help you see our new future."

—Seth Godin, author, *Linchpin*

"Winners in today's digital economy build authentic brands that consistently engage their customers through contextually relevant and authentic experiences. Market success requires an Engagement Economy mindset."

—R. "Ray" Wang, Principal Analyst & Founder,
Constellation Research, Inc.

"The most successful companies go beyond simply understanding 'who' their customers are to focus on identifying both preferences and priorities. *Engage to Win* dives deeper into this concept by delivering strategic guidance for how to execute this approach."

—Jamie Gutfreund, Global Chief Marketing Officer, Wunderman

"It's paradoxical how digitization has simplified so much but also resulted in massive complexity of choice and demands for our finite level of attention. The approach Steve Lucas sets out can help marketers be more impactful by moving from simply being the *loudest* to being the most *relevant and engaging* voice."

—Glenn Thomas, Chief Marketing Officer, GE Healthcare

"Successful, agile marketers are constantly focused on driving meaningful digital engagement with their customers. *Engage to Win* demonstrates how sharp marketers can engage more deeply across digital channels to ensure customers remain loyal across all micro moments."

—Kevin Wordon, Chief Digital Officer, Retail Food Group

ENGAGE TO WIN

A Blueprint for Success in the Engagement Economy

STEVE LUCAS

GREENLEAF
BOOK GROUP PRESS

This publication is designed to provide accurate and authoritative information in regard to the subject matter covered. It is sold with the understanding that the publisher and author are not engaged in rendering legal, accounting, or other professional services. If legal advice or other expert assistance is required, the services of a competent professional should be sought.

Published by Greenleaf Book Group Press
Austin, Texas
www.gbgpress.com

Distributed by Greenleaf Book Group

For ordering information or special discounts for bulk purchases, please contact Greenleaf Book Group at PO Box 91869, Austin, TX 78709, 512.891.6100.

Design and composition by Greenleaf Book Group
Cover design by Greenleaf Book Group

Publisher's Cataloging-in-Publication data is available.

Print ISBN: 978-162634-498-3

eBook ISBN: 978-1-62634-499-0

Part of the Tree Neutral® program, which offsets the number of trees consumed in the production and printing of this book by taking proactive steps, such as planting trees in direct proportion to the number of trees used: www.treeneutral.com

TreeNeutral

Printed in the United States of America on acid-free paper

18 19 20 21 22 23 24   10 9 8 7 6 5 4 3 2 1

First Edition

Dedicated to our customers, partners,
the passionate team of marketers at Marketo,
and my family, whom I treasure.

CONTENTS

FOREWORD

I've been a marketer for more than twenty years. In that time, the tools and responsibilities of the marketing role have shifted, but the backbone of our craft has remained the same—to connect consumers with brands. The rise of digital has radically shifted what this looks like. First, there were new channels: new places to reach consumers. Then, there were new technologies: new ways to reach consumers. This shift can be overwhelming, making it imperative that marketers look to partners that can help them navigate this new digital landscape.

One such partner is Marketo. During my time on the company's board, it became clear that Marketo wasn't only thinking about the technology that today's marketers are using, but how marketers and their companies can rethink the idea of connection. And, as I've learned during my time leading marketing for brands such as KidZania, Nintendo, Yahoo!, and Frito-Lay, connection and true engagement form the basis of successful organizations in this new digital age.

The concept of "engagement" that Steve lays out in the following pages resonated with me most, because it goes beyond the traditional buyer-seller dynamic. In writing my own book, *Fit Matters*, I sought to solve the dilemma of "fit" between employees and organizations. When employees feel disengaged at work, they're not set up for success. It's about the employees knowing what they need but also about employers understanding how best to engage them. You'll find a similar concept within *Engage to Win*; marketers and their organizations cannot expect to be successful until they understand the needs of their customers, prospects, partners, and employees.

That's why this book, and the idea of engagement as a driver of business success, resonates so significantly with me. I commend Steve for tackling this important topic and for emphasizing that engagement isn't just about buyers and sellers; it's about everyone. Steve addresses the topic from a unique perspective, having spent more than twenty-five years at enterprise software companies that engage a wide variety of stakeholders.

As you read through the following pages, you're going to be introduced to a new model for how marketers can not only exist but thrive in a new hyper-digital world—one founded on engagement. This digital era demands that marketers understand the science of marketing in order to scale and succeed, which is why Steve's direction on technology, metrics, and skill sets should be required reading for today's marketers.

I am thrilled to endorse this book and congratulate you on taking the first step on your own journey to Engage to Win.

—Cammie Dunaway, Global CMO, Board Member,
and author of *Fit Matters: How to Love Your Job*

PROLOGUE

This is all we do.

Before reading this book, it is fair of you to ask, "So, who is this guy, and why should I believe what he has to say?"

There are four reasons. Let's start with me and work outward to discuss Marketo.

Point number one. For the last twenty-plus years, I have become somewhat of an expert in data analysis and analytics. I've even authored multiple books on the topic. In all that time, what I've learned most about data analytics is that most people don't focus on data analytics.

The reality is that, as human beings, most of the time, we seek out information that validates our preconceived notions, not information that brings truth to a conversation, because that's often uncomfortable.

That leads us to point number two. I'm the CEO of the world's largest independent marketing automation technology brand, Marketo. Our company is solely focused on creating marketing solutions *for the marketer*. That is it. That's all we do, all the time. We create ROI for the marketer by enabling you to grow your brand, drive revenue, and prove impact.

Part of that brings us to point number three. Marketo has the world's largest online marketing community. We call it the Marketing Nation (https://www.marketo.com/why-marketo/marketing-nation/), and it is where more than 60,000 marketers from around the world come together to share information, for example, about best practices in selling to Millennials, marketing campaigns that worked—and those that didn't—and why, and debate ideas. I love that!

We don't own the community. Yes, we pay for the website. We certainly pay for the technology to facilitate the discussions, and we will submit our own content from time to time. And obviously, everyone at our company is exposed to the Marketing Nation every day. But we let the community self-organize around one concept: thought leadership in the world of engagement marketing.

Finally, one of the biggest perks of my job as CEO of Marketo is that I get to spend my days and nights talking to the world's leading thinkers in marketing—each of you. So, I am exposed constantly to the best of the best in the world of marketing every single day. I learn from you and hope to share these aggregate insights so that we can build on them together.

All my experience, observations, and conversations have convinced me that we must engage with—and not market to—our customers. Otherwise, our companies will eventually become irrelevant. In this book, we're going to introduce a new model for marketing as a whole—a model founded on engagement—along with suggesting new processes and many new ideas.

Engage to win!

INTRODUCTION

Overcoming the Laws that Govern
Our Marketing Universe

The law of supply and demand is sacred to us as marketers. We learn it from day one in school or at work, because it's our core. It applies to everything we do. As marketers, we think of ourselves as owning the demand side of the equation.

Over time, the demand we drive has evolved from one-to-one, to one-to-many, to a ratio today that would have been unthinkable even a decade ago. Our ability through technology to instantly tap into the collective consciousness of billions of people is, in a very real sense, the norm today. Realistically, who among us would have predicted ten years ago that:

- Facebook would have literally *billions* of active *daily* users? (I know somebody will claim to have called it, but it's safe to say that most people didn't.)

- A single e-commerce vendor like Amazon would process *tens of millions* of orders per *day?*

- A social media platform would allow people to share *tens of thousands* of 140-character comments per *second?*

Yet here we are, in the eye of an unprecedented storm of connected people and data. And from all this data, we can—leveraging marketing technology—create precise profiles of individual preferences and buying patterns on a global scale. We've harnessed the power of cloud technology to achieve unimaginable levels of reach and scale, and it may feel like we, as marketers, have an almost infinite supply of buyers for what we sell.

But the law of supply and demand, as governing as gravity, applies to human attention spans as well. The people (i.e., buyers we are trying to reach) have a finite amount of attention to give to any individual, brand, company, or organization. Furthermore, those slices of limited attention grow even thinner due to an ever-increasing demand for and on people's time.

The hyperscale we have created and the marketing technology we employ have forced buyers to be more careful today than ever before when it comes to lending *anyone* or *anything* their attention.

This may sound like I am asserting that attention is becoming a currency. I am. Because it is. Like anything else, attention is in finite supply and is being spent by customers as carefully as money. This macro trend will continue.

> This may sound like I am asserting that attention is becoming a currency. I am. Because it is.

This is a huge problem (and opportunity) for all of us who market for a living, and at the same time, it runs us smack into the second law that influences everything we do today: the law of diminishing returns. As marketers, not a day goes by where we aren't offered more tools we can leverage to appeal to a buyer's attention—even as our potential audience is spending less and less time considering what we have to say.

When a room becomes crowded and noisy, our natural response is to speak louder, even yell. Increasing our volume can have a positive effect—temporarily. But the increase in your decibel level forces others to increase theirs as well. The question to ponder is whether a continual increase in volume will garner the attention we need to build our brands and drive revenue. The short answer is no.

To be clear, this is not a condemnation of marketing technology—quite the opposite. It's an appeal to all marketers to leverage the technology available to us today and deliver more valuable engagement with our customers, prospects, employees, and partners. (More on this later.)

The point in this thread is that doing more of the same—sending more email, for example—won't move the needle past a certain point in a world of finite attention. In fact, the more stridently we speak, the more email we send, the more Tweets we push, and the more and louder we try to communicate all adds up to one inevitable conclusion: Our prospective buyers tune out. They just stop listening.

There's plenty of data to prove that assertion, yet I only need one data point to get you to agree with me: your own email inbox. Just think about how you as a consumer view your Gmail (or other) account. What's the value-to-spam ratio? 1 to 10? 1 to 100? Either way, consider how the volume of communication from a particular vendor affects your view of them.

Said another way, the more we push the *volume* of messages, touchpoints, content, apps, offers, etc., the less *valuable* each one becomes to the very people we are trying to reach, and value is the key to thriving in our high-scale, digital world.

The sole purpose of this book is to explain how you can provide more value to your existing and potential customers, thus raising their lifetime value for you and your organization.

ONE

Engage to Win

What you'll learn in this chapter:

- Why no one wants to be "marketed to" anymore.
- Why we find ourselves smack dab in the middle of the Engagement Economy.
- Why customers no longer just compare you to your competitors. (They also judge you against the best companies everywhere.)
- You need a new mantra: Listen, learn, engage.

You know this, but not everyone does: No one wants to be marketed to. No one. For proof, all we need do is look in the mirror.

Let's do a little more introspection. Do you enjoy those ads that follow you around the Internet, based on nothing more than something you searched for on Google *once*? How about the solicitations that clutter up a potentially interesting webpage or the ads that have nothing to do with your personal preferences and that—to make things worse—cover up content you'd like to read? Do you look forward to spam cluttering up your inbox? How about the constant, relentless messages from a retailer you once purchased something from months (or years) ago?

Is this the kind of marketing anyone wants? You don't. I don't. And neither do our prospects and customers. As humans—not marketers—who wakes up in the morning and thinks, *I want to be marketed to today!?*

Here's a simple, but pivotal question: Do you want to be marketed to or engaged with? (Hint: Your customers will make the same choice you did every time.)

However, if I asked, "Do you want to be engaged with?" you're probably going to say, "Yeah, I do. I do want to be engaged. I want someone to listen to me. I want to feel that my opinion matters. I like feeling wanted. I want to be understood and see the fact that I am valued reflected not only in the way I am treated but in the products and services I buy from you."

This is not just me talking. There's plenty of data to back me up. Wunderman, a leading digital agency that is part of WPP, one of the largest global communications companies, completed a survey[1] of consumers in the United States and the United Kingdom, investigating the buying behaviors of businesses (i.e., B2B marketing). Here's their big takeaway: "Brands must demonstrate at every step in the customer journey that they understand what consumers need and want. Some 79% of business buyers in the US and 72% in the UK said they would only consider brands that show they understand and care about them."

That's an amazing statement! More than seven of ten people surveyed said they will only consider brands that understand

---

1   Research conducted by Wunderman, a global digital agency that surveyed 1,000 people in the US and the UK in 2016

and care about them. And that wasn't in the B2C or consumer market; *this was B2B*—which I've been told is supposed to be a less "emotional" market.

That insight was confirmed by consumer and business purchasing data. Wunderman found that 89% of US customers and 84% in the UK "are loyal to brands that share their values." If you want proof of the power of engagement, you don't have to look any further.

There are two other things that jump out from the Wunderman research. The first: 88% of people in the US and 90% in the UK "want to engage with brands that are setting new standards." That sounds very B2C-ish, but the comment actually came from B2B buyers!

The final huge takeaway? Some 87% of people in the US and 85% in the UK said they don't measure brands against those brands' peers. Rather, they compare them to companies people perceive to have strong engagement practices, such as Amazon, Netflix, and Starbucks. As Wunderman put it, "You aren't just measured against your direct competitors anymore. You're stacked up against the best, regardless of industry."

We'll return to the Wunderman data later. For now, let me summarize it with one "macro" point: To win in today's world, we must move beyond marketing and engage. Because we are all living in a new era, one I call the *Engagement Economy*.

WHAT IS THE ENGAGEMENT ECONOMY?

The idea behind the Engagement Economy is simple but profound. We are living in a new era, a digital world where everyone and everything is connected, enabling changes in

(continued)

buyer sentiment literally second by second. This has caused a fundamental shift in relationships not only between buyers and sellers but across entire organizations. Customers, prospects, employees, and partners are also affected.

Why is this important? That's simple. The marketer in this new era must engage with all stakeholders in a business—not just the customer—and deliver an experience that resonates.

The organizations that do this will win, and those that fail to embrace this kind of transformation aren't long for this new world.

Today, the customer is in charge. The buyer—and to be clear, the buyers I am talking about are B2B customers and traditional consumers—is more informed than ever about your brand from search, social, blogs, video, and hundreds of additional digital touchpoints—very few of which you control. They are forming opinions, reaching conclusions, and influencing others well before you even have a chance to make your pitch.

A key point to understand here, and perhaps share with your peers, is that the buyer journey is highly fractured today. No one today in a B2B purchasing scenario simply calls up a salesperson they have no relationship with and buys something of value. A prospective customer today will have encountered literally hundreds of micro touchpoints throughout their buying journey, and it is the job of the marketer to ensure that each one of those experiences or touchpoints is engaging and meaningful.

If in your next marketing or sales planning meeting you see a "funnel" or journey model that looks like either of the ones following, then I can already tell you that change is needed!

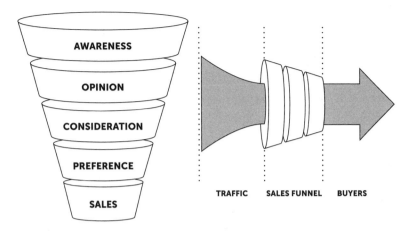

Figure 1.1 The dangers of assuming a customer journey is linear
can lead to poor decision-making.

Why? Because no matter how modern the picture looks, it's still a funnel, which implies there is an end to engagement.

These pictures are even more misleading because they lead senior management to believe that a buyer journey is linear, when it's not. A buyer journey today is non-linear and can involve dozens of physical and virtual influences, most of which are out of your control!

When I talk about engagement, I am referring to consistent engagement with your customers, prospects, employees, and partners in a meaningful manner across any channel where a buyer may experience your brand.

That's the way it is today—and things will only become more frenetically paced going forward. So, how do we win the heart and mind of the buyer in this new world? By developing a real strategy around engagement. We are starting to see examples of this working successfully all around us.

TOMS® Shoes has become incredibly successful, in large part because of what it stands for. You buy a pair, and the company donates a pair to underserved children. Simple. Everyone who wears TOMS shoes knows this. TOMS has built a movement and invited its customers to be a part of it.

Okay, fine. Marketing shoes isn't the same as marketing health insurance, and many people tend to view health insurance companies as largely the same as one another. But think about the differentiation that would occur, as well as the engagement, if your health insurance company sent you a note that said, "With your daughter turning 26 soon, she'll need her own insurance policy, and we have some options that will keep her covered and healthy." This sort of communication, as this message shows, doesn't have to be melodramatic. But a simple amount of proactivity demonstrating you understand a family's dynamics—and that you care—goes a long way.

Lyft is another great example. Perhaps trying to further differentiate itself from Uber, it alerted its riders to an upcoming feature dubbed "Round Up and Donate." "Opt in," Lyft wrote, "and we'll automatically round up your total fare to the nearest whole dollar and push the difference towards issues impacting everyone everywhere." This higher purpose is something many buyers like, especially as our marketing orients toward younger audiences.

Hopefully, the argument that we must engage people, not market to them, is starting to resonate. And we must engage them early, engage them everywhere, and do so in meaningful ways at all times.

The choice is binary. We can choose to engage, choose to demonstrate we understand the values of our buyer, and choose to let them know we want them as a customer, or we can be sentenced to a lifetime of irrelevance.

The choice is clear: Engage to win!

THE ONLY WAY FORWARD

It may sound simple, but very few organizations practice the following mantra: *Listen,* learn, and engage. If that methodology isn't embedded within your organization, you are sentencing yourself to irrelevance.

Rather than outlining an incredibly complex process for engaging with your customers, I'll boil it down to those three steps I just mentioned: Listen, learn, and engage. Their simplicity is the point. In my twenty-plus years in B2B sales and marketing, I have yet to encounter a company that has mastered the act of simply listening, learning, and engaging.

Let's take the steps one at a time.

In step 1, you need to listen to your customers and prospects, every minute of every day, forever. All too often in marketing, we want to get to the punch line and immediately tell everyone how wonderful our products and services are. Instead, try listening—really listening—not to just what someone wants from a product or service, but to who they are as a person. What's important to them? What do they care about? What matters to them? Only after you know these things do you ask how they like to be engaged. Texts? Videos? Emails? Social? At what times? What content and context appeals to them most, and what doesn't? While it sounds simple, effective listening can be the hardest thing that a marketer must do.

> It may sound simple, but very few organizations practice the following mantra: Listen, learn, and engage.

Then, you translate that listening into learning. That's step 2. You should be able to say, "After we talked to a lot of people, I heard potential customers say they want this; they don't like that. They like companies that do *x*; they hate companies that do *y*." Listening creates insights, and insights pave the way for engagement. Contrast that with marketing and sales planning meetings you sit in today. Most of the ones I've attended start and end with what someone wants to sell.

And then you take step 3 and engage, acting on what you've learned. Act on those insights by engaging with your buyers the way they want you to, when they want you to. Do this, and you will win the hearts and minds of those you are trying to connect with. And in the business and consumer worlds, that often translates into both short-term revenues and long-term loyalty.

Simply put, listening creates insights, insights drive engagement, and engagement drives revenue.

Again, the data bears this out. Marketo commissioned independent research[2] to survey both B2B and B2C customers around the world, and this is what respondents said:

- Two out of every three B2B customers want to advocate for brands that demonstrate they care about the customer.

- Half of consumers think vendors and brands could do a better job of aligning their engagement activities with how consumers prefer to engage with them.

- Three out of four B2B customers think vendors or brands must have a deep understanding of their needs to engage successfully.

So, if you've done steps 1 and 2 well, you'll know that the keys to engagement are these:

---

2 Commissioned third-party independent research firm Illuminas in March and April 2017. Respondents included more than 1,100 marketers in the United States, United Kingdom, France, and Germany, and more than 1,000 consumers—both B2B and B2C—from the US and UK

- Aligning what you do to your customers' personal and business values.

- Displaying and extending a feeling of truly wanting and needing that customer. You must show them you don't think they are dispensable.

- Creating the *experience* customers want. Allow your customers to interact with you and your company the way they want, when they want, at every part of the buying process. You must map and then align to the journey a customer wants to take or even allow them to self-define their journey on the road to doing business with you. You never dictate it.

Notice I said *every part* of the journey. As many organizations have learned the hard way, you can lose a customer—or fail to gain one—if they have a bad experience with your company at any time, in any way. Even when those experiences are with your legal, finance, or product management teams. That's why engagement, which should be led by the marketer, is not only a marketing thing. It's something that Quan Nguyen, Vice President of Marketing for Lennox Residential, part of the huge heating and manufacturing company Lennox, believes as well.

"Driving engagement has a lot to do with changing the company culture to be more customer-centric. This includes our credit, warranty, and administration teams. Currently, these teams do not believe they touch customers, but what they do really does impact customer experiences."[3]

When you do all this and do it well, your customer inevitably

---

3 Karen Steele, "Voices of the Engagement Economy: Quan Nguyen, VP of Marketing, Lennox Residential," CMO Nation (blog), https://cmo.marketo.com/2017/07/27/voices-engagement-economy-quan-nguyen-vp-marketing-lennox-residential/.

experiences a feeling about and passion for your product. Not only do they buy, but they also tell others. They become a *brand advocate.*

Brand advocates are the *nirvana* of marketing in the Engagement Economy. These are people you don't have to ask to promote your brand. You undoubtedly have some brand advocates today, driving some of your earned media coverage. To be clear, when we talk about brand advocates, we're talking about more than earned media—though it's important not to assume earned media and brand advocates are the same thing. Brand advocates are constituted primarily of customers, partners, and employees who willingly promote your brand on their own because of how strongly they feel connected to your offering. The most powerful organizations will be those that amass global forces of brand advocates who readily support and help see them through the ups and downs every company experiences.

That kind of backing is true engagement.

THERE IS NO ALTERNATIVE

Engagement distinguishes the best companies from everyone else. Aren't there other strategies besides engagement you can follow to be successful?

No, not really.

To show why that is the case, let's go back to the Wunderman research we mentioned earlier.

Wunderman's research said we are all measured not against our competition, but against the best of the best. Let's look at one of the superior companies that Wunderman singled out—Netflix—and see how they rose to the top.

Specifically, let's examine the classic example of Blockbuster Video versus Netflix to discover why. (I know you've heard this story before, but I promise we'll look at it from a completely new angle.)

> Engagement distinguishes the best companies from everyone else.

The whole reason Blockbuster died is because it made no attempt to understand and engage with its customers. None whatsoever.

Start with the way you got its product. The brand made you go to its stores. It was the biggest chain and, in theory, should have been the easiest way to rent a movie.

Once you got to the store—and going to the store was the only way to rent—the selection was limited. Blockbuster's "recommendation" engine for movies you might like was literally a sixteen-year-old behind the counter.

The checkout process was laborious. You had to queue up in long lines, because Blockbuster wanted to try to sell you microwave popcorn and Milk Duds® on the way to the register.

The reality is that whether you are buying as a consumer or you're buying for a business, engagement factors substantially into the decision. People want relationships—personalized, meaningful, and authentic relationships—with the companies that they do business with.

When it came time to return the movie, you had to drive back to the store. If you were late, the penalties were severe—a percentage of the cost of the rental—and on top of that, Block-buster wanted you to rewind the film for it. (Yes, my Millennial friends, rewinding was a thing we had to do.) So, the only engagement Blockbuster had with you was negative. That was how it engaged: badly!

Before we get to Netflix, I think it's important for us to

contemplate if there are Blockbuster trappings in our own companies. If any of the deficiencies I just laid out in Blockbuster's business model resonates vis-à-vis your existing company, it's time to change! Now, on to Netflix.

Netflix turned every single negative experience from Blockbuster on its head, and in the process of doing so, created a "closed-loop" experience, where much of the traditional marketing its competitors did was actually *part of the product* itself. You never had to go to the store. Even when Netflix's business model was just sending DVDs through the mail, every bit of inventory was visible with a few clicks of your mouse. The selection was virtually unlimited. It offered algorithm-based movie recommendations. Heck, Netflix even held a contest calling on the public to help it build the best content recommendation algorithm possible. The winner got $1 million (a brilliant PR move). And you could return the DVDs whenever you wanted. Not only was there no late fee, Netflix paid the postage both ways.

It is important to understand what Netflix did so that you can do it too.

It used technology to drive engagement, number one.

And number two, it ruthlessly dissected the Blockbuster model, understood acutely all those negative engagement points—limited selection, no recommendations, requiring you to go to the store *twice* for each rental, etc.—and turned each and every one of them into positives.

Netflix never once stopped digitally engaging with its customers and has since successfully built on that approach by moving to offer all forms of digital content, expanding into original television, movie programming, and more. It is planning on spending over $6 billion dollars on original content in the next few years! It is a true entertainment and engagement powerhouse. Netflix continues to evolve and continues to reinforce positive engagement with its customers. That's why it won against Blockbuster and continues to win today.

As I write this, Netflix has a market cap of more than $137 billion, or more than six times that of CBS.[4]

While the story isn't new, what fascinates me about it is how obvious the conclusions are, yet Blockbuster wasn't listening, learning, and engaging. In other words, it couldn't see a single step past its business model.

And it failed.

THE NEW RULES OF ENGAGEMENT

1. **Listen.** Develop the discipline of really listening to your customers.

2. **Learn** to take all that data you gather from customers and potential customers, and turn it into insights.

3. **Act** (i.e., **Engage**) on those insights, by dealing with your customers the way they want you to, when they want you to.

4. Never **forget** you don't create the engagement process; your customers do.

5. Don't **let anyone other than you** define what your organization stands for.

(continued)

---

4   https://www.google.com/search?rlz=1C1GCEA_enUS779US779&ei=r-
w6oWrSzOITUjwTQ_4rYAQ&q=netflix+market+cap&oq=netflix+market+-
cap&gs_l=psy-ab.3..0i131k1j0l9.6837.13581.0.13907.11.11.0.0.0.0.189.1073
.9j2.11.0..2..0 . . . 1.1.64.psy-ab..0.11.1072 . . . 0i273k1.0.f_sbvb2Bnbc

6. Everyone **in the company** has the opportunity to influence the engagement process—for good or evil. Choose good.

7. **Guard content with your life** as none of your outbound content, whether an email, a video, whatever, should ever leave your company without being vetted by some type of focus group or feedback pool. In today's age of hyper-reactivity, this is a must.

8. Never **assume that what you knew to be true yesterday** is true today. The world is evolving at an unprecedented, accelerated pace in terms of norms, tastes, preferences, beliefs, biases, and on and on and on.

ONE LAST THOUGHT ABOUT THIS

We touched on this a bit earlier, but it's worth revisiting one last time. I don't know when the tipping point happened, but in today's world, there is no amount of money that any company on the planet possesses that would enable it to outspend its customers' voice. It's impossible. If you factor in Facebook, Twitter, and the rest of social media, which have amplified word-of-mouth, it is simply impossible. Your marketing budget could be equal to the GDP of the United States and China *combined*, and it still would not be enough to outspend the voice of the buyer!

If an employee of a company makes an ill-advised Tweet or an organization like a bank gets caught doing something unethical relative to its customers, it can't control the situation. All it can try to do is limit the damage.

To be clear, this doesn't mean that branding is dead, or

that you shouldn't spend money on your brand. *Of course,* you should. But it means that the way you spend that money needs to profoundly change from the days when you controlled the message. Your organization must evolve to speak the language of your customer, align to your customers' values, and eliminate messaging that doesn't resonate. You have no choice. You may not like it, but the customer today has a more powerful voice than you.

If you recognize, accept, and, indeed, embrace that fact, it can be an extremely good thing. Bringing a level of humanity and soul to your products and to how you engage with people will cultivate brand advocates, who will continually promote and even *forgive* when you make mistakes. That powerful voice of the customer can make your organization stronger.

TWO

The Challenge We All Face

What you'll learn in this chapter:

- How to engage.
- How to synthesize quantitative and qualitative information about your customers and prospects.
- A new metric that will make your marketing more precise: Key Personal Value Indicators.
- The yin and the yang of customer retention.
- Why good enough never is.
- Why we are thinking about transformation the wrong way.
- How antiquated business model "lock-in" invariably causes not only frustration but also financial hardship.
- Why transformation is even harder than you think— and what you can do to simplify things.

EMPATHY

I want to underscore something here at the beginning of this chapter. You'll notice that I called it "the challenge we all face." The "we" is extremely important. The word "we" means we are all in this together, and that perspective is vital.

A key element of engagement is empathy, identifying with the thoughts and feelings of others. Your family and friends want to know that you understand what they are going through.

Your customers do as well. In every part of every interaction we have with them, we need to demonstrate that we are on the same side. Because this point is important, not only am I going to refer to it several times in the book, I wanted to mention it early on.

LAYING THE GROUNDWORK FOR ENGAGEMENT

Engagement, as we established, is understanding who your customer, consumer, or client is as a person and what they value. Before you can ever engage, you also need to know who you are talking to and the different channels by which you'll converse (e.g., inbound and outbound, digital and analog). You get the idea.

MARKETERS ARE BEGINNING TO ENGAGE

I was pleasantly surprised when our research revealed that most marketers have begun to understand the importance of engagement and that the best companies have already taken steps to make it a reality.

The data shows that marketers are investing in engagement primarily to retain existing customers (65%), meet increasing customer demands (57%), and respond to competitive market pressure (49%), which includes, in part, the fact that their peers are already doing this.

Two out of five companies are investing to build emotional connections to the brand, and one out of three are making investments to build brand advocates of their customers.

It seems so obvious, yet most of the time, most companies deal with people as if they are anonymous IP addresses. Our culture has become *hyper-transactional*. Granted, it's much more pronounced in developed nations, but the point is that our society is optimized entirely for efficiency, so we simply do not know enough about our customers, and our customers agree that is the case. According to Marketo's independent research:

- 69% of buyers believe "engagements are relevant but still primarily transactional."

- Just 16% said that "brands take the time to understand me and develop a relationship." Even worse,

- 14% feel "like [they are] just being marketed to."

The key point here is that engagement begins with knowing who you're talking to and knowing some intimate level of detail about their likes, their wants, their hopes, their aspirations, and their dreams, not just their preferences. You may think that you do this today (i.e., you've developed a buyer persona) but I will address this in more detail throughout the book. We must go beyond a basic demographic representation of an ideal or even real customer and get into granular levels of detail about our customers and prospects that will enable us to engage like never before. Admittedly this is difficult, but it's critical. Why? You can't infer that because I bought a tent on Amazon, I like camping. It could be that I'm buying it for my brother-in-law, who is an outdoor enthusiast. The algorithm doesn't know who I'm buying the tent for. It just knows that I'm buying it. Using science alone to figure out what your customer wants can lead you astray.

Since engagement is about delivering personal and authentic experiences, the first thing you'll need to do is build a *digital* persona (i.e., a digital profile of every customer or prospect you intend to do business with). A digital persona goes way beyond demographics and gets into much more fine-grained, deterministic data. To be precise, a *digital* persona is a data-driven model of someone that contains both quantitative and qualitative information about them, especially as it relates to that person's online behavior.

**CUSTOMER AND PROSPECT
DIGITAL PERSONA DATABASE**

QUANTITATIVE

Personal Data
Demographic Data
Household Data
Transaction History
Browsing History
...

QUALITATIVE

Lifestyle
Social Identity
Family Influence
Brand Preference
Social Graph
Aspiration
Communication Preference
Media Preference
...

Figure 2.1 Most marketing contact databases contain quantitative data but often lack qualitative data that facilitates better engagement.

The second most important thing you can do is determine the what, the when, and the how of engagement (i.e., how you can deliver the right message at the right time). This is where you start mapping out inbound and outbound activity and aligning it with your current and potential customers.

An easy way to do that is simply to ask a customer, "How should I be engaging with you? By phone? In person? Digitally? All the above? When should I be engaging with you? (For example, if you want me to engage digitally, when should I send emails?) And who do you want to be doing the engaging? Account executives? Customer success managers?"

It's impossible to engage if you don't know the person you're talking to. And unfortunately, the reality today is that most organizations have no idea who they're talking to. Before you can even engage, you must attempt to better understand who you are communicating with. You need to develop a digital persona of your buyer.

Third, when you do engage, you need to know your prospect's or customer's mood. Most companies today don't really take the time to try and sense your mood, and that's a mistake. Why? Because you may not *be* in a buying mood! How many times have you had an off-putting experience when you're not in a buying mood, but someone is really trying to sell you something—whether you're sitting at your desk browsing a website, you're physically in the mall, or you're sitting in a park using a mobile app? To some degree, mood can be inferred by probabilistic means or data, as it's not an exact science.

What is mood in an economic sense? It's a propensity to buy at a given point. It's the difference between "kicking the tires" and actually buying a car. And yes, you can "sense" mood digitally. But let's start with an analog example.

I always think about the three kinds of people in a shopping mall. There are those who are there to walk around, those who are window shopping (i.e., not really buying anything), and then there are others who are there to buy something, anything. You need to know who you are dealing with.

If you understand someone's mood, you can understand their intent to buy. And as I said, *you absolutely can understand mood digitally.* Most digital marketers today can get a sense for whether someone is just "clicking" around. We know how much time they are spending on a page and understand their browsing behavior. Incredible advances in marketing applications are based on Artificial Intelligence (AI) that, through sophisticated data analysis and modeling, can determine if someone is ready to buy.

Does mood only matter in a B2C setting as opposed to B2B? No: It's vital to understand in B2B settings as well. Here's why. Let's say you are a software company and provide a cloud product. If someone lands on your site for the first time, you most likely don't know that person. They're an unknown IP address, and if they are like you and me, they'll use multiple devices, so they may visit you in the morning from an iPhone and in the afternoon from a desktop. Furthermore, you don't know if that person is a buyer or someone simply researching your offering. This is where the audience data you collect, how you classify it, and then continue to refine it over time matters most.

On the other hand, in a B2C scenario, if someone visits the Under Armour® website to look at running gear, for example, they've come specifically to the website for a particular item. Knowing that fact is far more valuable than knowing that someone on Amazon.com was looking at thirty different brands of jogging pants.

In our example, our buyer has landed on a preferred brand site—www.underarmour.com. They're specifically looking at jogging pants, and then they're specifically evaluating things like color. The question that you have to ask at that micromoment as a retailer is, "Is my job to educate the buyer? Or is my job to incent the buyer to purchase now? What am I trying to do?"

And the reality is that, for any retailer, you can go about it the right way, or you can go about it the wrong way. You might go about it in a way where you could potentially turn off the buyer, and you clearly don't want to do that. Knowing *what* to do in that moment is what engagement is all about. You want to deliver the right message at the right time.

KEY PERSONAL VALUE INDICATORS CAN HELP

A new marketing metric that helps you employ the engagement philosophy is Key Personal Value Indicators (KPVI).

A KPVI is not an industry-defined term. If you Google it, you will get "key *performance* value indicators," as in how I measure your performance as an employee. That's not what I'm talking about.

KPVIs boil down to an easy question to ask but a tough one to answer: What qualitative things define a customer?

As I mentioned earlier, most companies focus on the demographic details or basic quantitative data. You're five feet ten and *x* years old. You generally buy at this time of the day, week, or month. These are your preferences in terms of clothing type. Those are not *value* metrics. Those are just metrics.

The key personal values for me would be: Steve is a type one diabetic. He is health conscious. He's worried his kids will develop type one diabetes. He's a frequent exerciser who prefers CrossFit. He donates time and money to the American

Diabetes Association and Children's Diabetes Foundation.
Those are some, but not all, of *my* KPVIs.

With KPVIs as background, you can start asking questions.
Is Steve more likely to buy because a company indicates that
it recycles? Is he more likely to buy because an organization
makes a charitable donation on his behalf? Knowing someone's key personal values can allow you to ask those kinds of
questions. And those values will lead you down the path of creating higher customer lifetime value, because you will be able
to truly engage with the person you are trying to reach.

You may be sitting there thinking that Key Personal Value
Indicators are too qualitative. And while there are, indeed,
qualitative notions baked into KPVIs, the truth is, we need to
understand them now more than ever. Yes, they go *way* beyond
the 4Ps of marketing—product, price, place, and promotion—
that we learned. But isn't the Engagement Economy, the world
you live in today, way beyond the one you grew up in?

For a moment, I'd like to return to an example I used
earlier: TOMS Shoes. (Note: This isn't a double-blind study
conducted by an independent research firm.) I was being inter-
viewed by six reporters—four men and two women—at an
industry tradeshow, and I decided to ask them a question. "Do
any of you own a pair of TOMS shoes?"

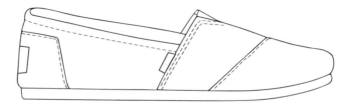

Figure 2.2 A replica of a TOMS shoe.

Both women raised their hands. (TOMS sells shoes for men,
women, and kids.)

I said, "Okay, what happens when you purchase one pair of TOMS shoes?" They both said, "TOMS donates a second new pair to someone who needs shoes." They immediately knew TOMS' value proposition.

"Now, let me ask you a second question," I said. "Do you consider TOMS shoes to be the most attractive pair of shoes in your wardrobe?" They both said no. On a scale of 1 to 10, with 10 being most attractive, one gave TOMS a two, the other a three. So, clearly the attractiveness of the shoe was not driving their decision to buy.

"Now, tell me about comfort." They both said, "They're super comfortable."

"But are they the most comfortable shoes you own?" They both said no and mentioned other brands.

Notice what is going on here. Both women said TOMS does not make the most comfortable pair of shoes, and they don't make their most attractive pair either, yet each of them had purchased multiple pairs. Clearly, *TOMS has aligned with their personal values.*

There are two important questions to ask when it comes to engagement marketing:

- How do I discover what is meaningful to you in your life?
- How do I relate my brand to that?

Knowing someone's KPVIs is extremely helpful, and the reason is obvious. In the Engagement Economy, there are just as many (if not more) things you can do to turn a buyer off as you can do to turn a buyer on. You only need to watch the news or skim social media to know that aligning to your customers' values is paramount.

United Airlines is a great example. By now, most of us are familiar with the situation where a passenger was forcefully removed from a United flight after refusing to give up his seat. While there are too many problems with that situation to analyze in this book, it was clear that United's insensitivity toward a customer made us all feel that we could one day be treated that way. United's image suffered dramatically as a result.

The point is that value alignment and good behavior aren't just digital acts but practices we as marketers need to champion everywhere. Brands that understand their customers' personal value indicators, and align their products and services to them, will win. And the ones that don't will lose.

ONE MORE THOUGHT ABOUT THIS

At the end of the day, engagement is not a unilateral or siloed way of thinking. Too many organizations get caught up in, "Well, we'll overstaff our stores with people on the sales floor so that we make sure we're engaging our customers." That is not engagement. Engagement is not a brute force act. Engagement is sophisticated. It is elegant. It is thoughtful in the how, the what, the when, the why of meaningful engagement overall. It's high-value added, and it's something that takes a lot of experimentation to get right.

But when you get it right, as TOMS does, it is a very powerful force. For good.

THE OPPOSITE OF ENGAGEMENT

I am and have been a member of the board of many different corporations and non-profits. At one board meeting, I had the unexpected chance to contemplate the difference between an *impression* and *engagement.*

The organization's CMO was presenting his case for additional funding based on what he said was the stellar performance of his department over the past several quarters. In fact, he highlighted a campaign that he cited as generating "billions" of impressions. That's "BILLIONS" with a big giant "B."

An impression—which is sometimes called an "ad view" or "view"—is the number of times an ad, page, email, or Tweet (for example) is seen or displayed on a webpage.

I listened to this person assert the "billions" figure, and I immediately thought, "Okay, first, there are only seven billion people on the planet. Second, let's pretend for a moment that you actually did create billions of impressions. Tell me, were those all *good* impressions? In other words, did they help create the outcome you wanted?"

It sure didn't look that way. His sales growth was meager.

Many marketers rely on impressions, opens, and click-through rates—the percentage of people seeing an ad who open it—to indicate levels of success relative to a campaign. But they shouldn't. They should be looking at the *rate of engagement* or the *number of brand advocates* they create and the number of people who are shouting from the mountaintops, "I love this company" as a result of their marketing efforts.

I get it. It's exciting to say, "We created a billion impressions!" But the reality is, there's no way to measure ROI from

(continued)

an impression without nearly flawless attribution data, and that is very difficult to come by.

The next time someone presents the number of impressions created by a campaign, ask them how many *bad* impressions were generated—how many of those impressions might have turned off a potential customer. My bet is the person won't know.

THE OTHER SIDE: EXPERIENCE

Engagement is just half of the success equation. No matter who you are trying to reach, engagement without a superior experience falls short.

Figure 2.3 The yin and yang of customer retention.

Think back to products like the CD player or the fax machine. It's not that those technologies were irrelevant. The fact that you recognize every one of them shows that they once *were* relevant. Highly relevant in fact! But relevance alone doesn't matter. Whether a product or service lasts comes down to how engaging you find it and your experience using it. It's not one or the other. It's both. They are the yin and yang of the Engagement Economy. Even someone who is extremely loyal to a product will walk away if the experience isn't right. You may love a specific retailer, but if its digital experience is a nightmare, and you do a significant percentage of your buying online, eventually you'll shop somewhere else.

THINGS CHANGE

Just because you have both the engagement and the experience right doesn't mean you are done.

Nothing stays the same forever, and you need to evolve as well.

Do you like listening to music? The compact disc player introduced by Sony in 1982 (at a cost of $900 then; equivalent to $2,300 in 2017) was once state of the art. Now it's perplexing, even tainting, to find a CD player included as part of a new car's sound system. While the experience was state of the art fifteen years ago, that same experience today can demean a brand.

From the engagement side, think about the United Airlines example we mentioned a bit earlier. Even extremely brand loyal United flyers posted pictures of their cut-up rewards cards on social media to protest United's handling of the incident.

In fact, it is becoming progressively easier to turn a buyer off.

Say the CEO of a company takes a political stand that most of her customers don't like. Whether she supported Donald Trump in the presidential election or not, it's a polarizing issue. Buyers will connect values with brands by inference, and many will choose to spend their money elsewhere. Buyers today want to know that the brands they are aligned with

(continued)

share their values. The moment those brands don't align, buyers will disengage and move on.

That brings me to a related point. Knowing your customers' values is not sufficient. You need to change as they do. The Earth's environment didn't used to be top of mind; today it is. Income inequality wasn't something many people thought about. Today a significant percentage of female buyers won't purchase goods or services from companies where a gender pay gap exists.

If you don't keep up with what is important to your customers, you can easily fall out of favor—and that is a point many people miss.

Author's disclosure: My personal preference is to buy things from companies that "do the right thing." If I believe a company doesn't treat people fairly, I don't buy from them!

What most people don't realize is that engagement is an ever-changing process. You can't just take a snapshot of what a customer thinks or what someone wants, draw a conclusion, and then move on. You have to constantly measure your customers' values, their wants, their needs, their desires relative to the journey that they want to have, and as a result of what you learn, you need to constantly fine-tune *your* business and *your* values.

If it sounds hard, it is. But this is what it takes to win people's minds *and* hearts!

This is why both engagement *and* experience are paramount. You can't have one without the other and be successful. A company that is hyper-focused on its customer and deeply understands who its clients and prospects are but hasn't nailed the experience will eventually fail. So too will companies with great products who don't get engagement.

If you get both, like Amazon does, you become "hyper" dominant.

To see why this is the case, let's first discuss the engagement Amazon provides and begin with its awareness of your preferences. This is obvious, but when you walk into a big box retailer, when do you swipe your customer loyalty card? *At the end*, which is the exact opposite of what you do when you visit Amazon.com or use the Amazon app. Amazon knows who you are when you "walk" into its store (i.e., log in).

The big box retailer has no chance to tell you about personalized offers as you walk into the store. Amazon, of course, can tell you about its specials the moment you log onto the site.

So, even before you start shopping, Amazon is ready to engage with you, and it does. It shows your order history, likes and dislikes, recommendations for you, and so on. With an Amazon Dash Wand (Google it), you can simply scan items around your house. And with Alexa, you can say out loud the items you need, and they are added to your online cart. Then, you can visit Amazon.com or the mobile app any time and pick up where you left off. "Your Amazon.com" suggests items based on what you bought in the past.

That level of engagement extends beyond your own behavior. You'll find "People who looked at what you did also bought X, Y, and Z." That creates a sense of belonging, even the tacit notion of "community," which engenders trust.

These sorts of things do not happen at a big box retailer. It could, I guess, if those retailers had knowledgeable staff in sufficient numbers to point out to you—and in some cases put in your hands—something they think you would like based on their past interactions with you. But neither of those things exist at most stores today.

That puts traditional retailers at a huge disadvantage and further cements Amazon's edge. Think about every big box retailer you have visited. You walk in. You are probably shopping for a specific thing. You search the store for it and often have a hard time finding it. You either buy, or you don't. There is little—if any—engagement during the process. Sure, someone may have greeted you as you walked in the door, welcoming you to the store. And if you did find one item on your list, the cashier may ask if you found everything you were looking for. But the opportunity for engagement has passed, because by this point, you're frustrated by your experience with this retailer.

Don't get me wrong. I am not anti-retail stores. I think there are products and specialty stores where the experience *is* the visit. Clothing is an example. And Apple stores are not hurting for traffic either. It's just that I believe big box retailers aren't doing enough to drive both the engagement and experience that will enable them to survive the Amazon "Age." That long list of negative engagement points I mentioned earlier just flat out turns buyers off.

What Amazon does is simple: It clearly understands the painful parts of the retail experience and makes them positives (just as Netflix did). You can find the products you are looking for easily. In addition to the products, you can see ratings and reviews from people who bought what you are looking at. Amazon is engaging as you shop. They make returns easy. Try returning something to Big Box with the long lines, unhelpful people, and restocking fees. With Amazon, you don't have to wait to check out or even pull out your credit card. There is a long list of things it has perfected as part of the experience. If you buy a complex product from Amazon, it offers an option for someone to set it up or install it for you. (I did this with a flat screen TV mount recently; it was a flawless experience!) It even offers a fixed price for the installation.

Ten years from now, there won't be any big box retailers in

the US, unless they can find a way to engage their buyers and provide a better experience.

If you're a B2B marketer, you may be thinking this scenario doesn't apply to you. I think it does. Are you a big box retailer from a bygone era or Amazon.com?

HOW DID WE GET HERE?

How did we get into this situation?

The answer is simple and has three parts.

First is the control of information.

Buyers are more informed and better informed than ever. Even before their initial conversation with you, they know an incredible amount about both your company and your offering thanks to the availability of virtually endless digital content, blogs, social media, and apps.

The most influential information-dissemination organizations in the world, like it or not, are Google, Facebook, Twitter, Snapchat, Instagram and the like. And most of them aren't even fifteen years old yet, so this powerful phenomenon is relatively new.

The second reason for the shift of power is the brand advocate. As a reminder, this is someone who is such a big fan of your brand that they voluntarily sing your proverbial praises to all the people in their social network.

Let's say that a particular brand advocate has one hundred followers on Twitter or one hundred friends on Facebook, and he tells them all about a wonderful experience he had with a brand. Now, let's play six degrees of separation. His contacts (those one hundred different people) repeat his story one hundred times each through each degree. By the time we are six steps removed from the original person, the message has been repeated one trillion times! That means a person with just one hundred contacts on Facebook has the ability to create a message that is echoed 133 times for everyone on Earth![1] I realize this is hyperbole taken to the furthest of extremes, but it underscores the point that the brand advocate is a powerful force!

Brand advocates voluntarily promote your brand online at little to no cost, providing a higher return on your marketing investment than just about anything else you can think of.

The third reason involves the rise of digitally "native" organizations, as well as the digital transformation that more established companies are pursuing.

A couple of things happen as companies accelerate and change their business activities, processes, competencies, and models to not only take advantage of but also fully exploit everything modern digital technology and cloud solutions offer.

The first is that digital natives provide a simpler solution that provides better engagement and experience. Think Uber, Airbnb, Instagram, Snapchat, and whatever else launched between me writing this book and it being published.

The second is this: As all the paper inside a company is digitized, just about all of it becomes available to customers and consumers. It has become remarkably easy to learn a lot about

---

1   The math is fun to do and fairly straightforward. A person with 100 contacts, playing Six Degrees of Separation, reaches 1,000,000,000,000 people. (100 × 100 × 100 × 100 × 100 × 100 = 1,000,000,000,000.)

a company—including the intricate details of its products or services—very quickly online. Yes, this can be risky, as internal presentations and documents are regularly shared on wikis and the like. But in the plus column, when is the last time you felt the need to keep a paper copy of an owner's manual? It's as if the skies have opened and dropped as much information as any buyer could possibly want right into their lap.

So, to sum up, digital transformation certainly is an aspect of what has changed. I believe social media has had possibly the largest impact of all. And of course, consumers and buyers self-educating themselves has altered our landscape forever.

WHAT THE DIGITAL TRANSFORMATION IS TRANSFORMING

Academics define digital transformation as "the acceleration in efficiency creation in business activities, business processes, and models to leverage digital technologies and their impact."

The rest of us would say digital transformation is all about using the latest technology to allow our companies and employees to do things better, faster, and cheaper.

There are different motivators for digital transformation. Sometimes it comes from a startup that wants to disrupt the way business is done in a certain industry. It sees an inefficiency in a process or a broken organizational model and chooses to disrupt by doing things in a dramatically different way. That's what Uber, Airbnb, and Instagram did, for example.

Uber especially stands out to me, because it disrupted the ride-sharing industry by leading a digital transformation based entirely on engaging with the customer to create a great experience.

With Uber, you can summon a ride almost anywhere in

the world from your mobile phone at any hour of the day or night. Uber never closes. And the process is remarkably easy. You don't have to tell the driver where to pick you up; your phone knows where you are. In fact, it not only knows where you are, but based on your history, it knows the spots that you prefer to visit, at what time you frequent them, and it knows the types of transportation that you prefer.

Even if you don't compete with Uber or you aren't in the transportation industry, your customers *still expect* this kind of experience from you.

Uber's engagement is excellent as well. After you summon your car, you never have to wonder where it is or when it will pick you up. You can track its progress as it works its way to you. That relieves potential stress. The engagement continues to work well when you are done with your trip. You just get out. There's no cash or credit card to hand over. There's no transaction. There's no nothing. You just get a perfectly crafted email that is ready for an expense report.

Plus, the pricing is transparent. It is based on demand, and you are never surprised. I was in Australia booking an Uber to the airport when I received a note from Uber that said, "It's high demand. Fares are going to be 2.2x their normal rate." What really caught my eye was that Uber wasn't afraid to say, "Fares will be high based on demand." It used that exact language and added, "Your trip could be expensive. Do you want to continue?"

What was interesting was my response. In a situation like that, the normal consumer reaction would be, "Wait a minute—you guys are ripping me off!" But because Uber was transparent and offered me the choice to continue, I said to myself, "Yeah. I want to continue. I appreciate you giving me that notice so I'm not looking at my follow-up email thinking, '*What the heck? How come the ride was more than twice what it usually was?*'"

Uber turned what could have been a negative experience and a negative engagement into a positive one. It is the kind of approach that is needed as we deal with transforming our organizations.

LOCKED INTO OLD THINKING

Today, there are thousands of massive organizations that are set in their ways and just flat out lack the ability or capacity to change easily. This is especially true for analog companies, but you can find the same problem emerging in the (now) aging and larger digital native firms as well.

These organizations want to transform the way they do business so that they can become more efficient and nimble, but because of the complexity of their business processes, or simply their size, they can't adapt to the changing needs of their customers quickly enough.

By way of example, let's go back to the Netflix versus Blockbuster scenario we covered in chapter 1. Before Netflix came along, what was so hard about sending someone a DVD in the mail?

Nothing . . . which is the fascinating part.

But because of the way Blockbuster was built—with freestanding stores that required substantial foot traffic to keep them profitable—the company could not get its head around the fact that people might want to rent DVDs by mail. I spoke to a former Blockbuster executive who said that Blockbuster was aware of the threat Netflix represented but considered the experience of renting a DVD by mail "sub-par." It thought a more engaging experience was the dazzle of a Blockbuster store with licorice and Milk Duds. At least we know Blockbuster was right about the duds.

(continued)

Staying with movies, think about Redbox, which rents videos through a vending machine. It took the Blockbuster model and shrunk it down to the size of a vending machine and then put the machines where people go. Grocery stores, McDonald's, Starbucks, Walgreens.

Even though Redbox is still around today, you can safely predict it will go out of business. Why? Because all the same problems you had with Blockbuster exist with Redbox as well. Just in a tiny red box. It's just preposterous to think that it lacks digital content delivery. Eventually, reality will catch up with it.

It's not hard to find other examples. How is it possible Tesla can even exist, let alone thrive? (I love Tesla, by the way, and own one, so stay with me on this.) First of all, you've got GM, Ford, Toyota, Honda, and all of the other well-established dominant automobile companies out there. So, how is there room for Tesla in a marketplace that is shrinking as more and more people decide they can live without owning a car?

The second question is, "How is it physically possible that Tesla, from an electric standpoint, can manufacture a vehicle superior to anything that any traditional automotive company can produce?" Is it really that hard? What we are talking about is nothing more than batteries, electric motors, and software. Is it that fundamentally difficult for the major players to do it?

It's not. But because of their existing business processes, the older car companies cannot react in an agile and relevant manner to create an engaging experience for the consumer.

Think about Chevrolet's launch of the Volt. Chevy introduced the Volt in 2015, which was late to the party, and it had a forty-mile range. It could only go a total of forty miles without requiring recharging. Who on God's green earth is going to buy a car with a forty-mile range? No one. And the sales numbers proved it. GM's former CEO, Dan Akerson, publicly predicted sales of 60,000 Volts per year. The company ended up delivering roughly 76,000 Volts in four years.[2]

A base model Tesla, on the other hand, will go 215 miles between charges, and the research shows that 200 is the minimum magic number. Consumers want a car that can do a 200-mile round trip without the need for being plugged in.

Was GM lacking that data? No. It knew exactly what the magic number was. But it ignored it. So, when it brought its product to market, it didn't have any relevance to the consumer because of the Volt's limited range. It fundamentally lacked engagement.

Why would GM make such a flawed decision? It had to compromise on what it offered, because the only way it could make money on the car was to include a gas engine that would kick in when the Volt ran out of electric power, as it invariably would. GM was forced to include a gas motor in the design of its electric car because of its business model. Without including—and charging for—the gas motor, the Volt was not a profitable proposition.

Author's note: Just about the time this book went to press, Chevy finally launched the Bolt (not the Volt), which is an all-electric car with a 200-mile minimum range. While this is redemptive for Chevy, the company is not seen as the thought or innovation leader in the electric vehicle (EV) segment.

---

2   The Truth About Cars (http://www.thetruthaboutcars.com/2015/05/first-generation-volt-success-failure/).

CUSTOMER ENGAGEMENT NEEDS TO BE AT THE HEART OF TRANSFORMATION

Nearly every enterprise company is either in the process of transforming its business (digitally) or soon will be. That's true whether you work for a more established company, one that was in business before the Internet existed, or for my digital native company. That is, an organization that was born online and whose business model, revenue, retention, and overall engagement with customers is predicated on cloud software and digital devices, such as mobile phones and apps.

Invariably, as companies undergo this transformation, they put in place what they think are the necessary systems and processes to operate in a new, more agile, and improved manner. Only then (typically) do they try to figure out the best way to engage customers and prospects going forward.

That is backward.

First, you need to define your engagement outcome; figure out the outcome you want your customers to feel and experience as they engage with you. Only then do you put the new organization in place to allow that to happen. Taking those steps, in that order, is the only way successful and lasting transformation can occur.

SIMPLE. BUT NOT EASY.

The key questions to ask about transformation are these: "How do I radically simplify my organization, and how do I remove complexity from my business processes to respond both faster and better to my customers?"

Let's walk through the answer to those questions for both analog and digital companies.

The reality is that for the non-digital native, complexity has had a big head start. In the case of an established firm, it may have a head start for hundreds of years. Literally. American companies like Cigna, Dixon Ticonderoga, and Jim Beam are now more than 200 years old. For analog companies, engaging with customers is more difficult, because, compared to a digital firm, they generally have less information about who is buying their product.

Digital companies find it relatively easy to identify customers and capture data beyond IP addresses, such as device ID and email address. In contrast, an analog company may get paid in cash. It may operate through a reseller or some third-party distributor that doesn't provide them transaction-level insight, let alone information at all, about a buyer. The reality is that an analog company may be either blind to information about its customers or have an incomplete view.

Let's take a simple example. It's B2C-ish, but I like the metaphor, because I like grilling.

If you buy a grill, you probably don't buy it directly from the manufacturer (we will call the real, well-established company I am going to describe GrillCo to disguise it). Can you buy a GrillCo grill online? Absolutely. But a majority of GrillCo's revenue comes through massive distribution agreements with strong-arm retailers, so odds are you get it at Home Depot or Lowe's or maybe your local hardware store. So, GrillCo probably doesn't know who you are.

It's like what happens when I shop at my local supermarket. When it is time for me to check out, I'm always asked for my loyalty card, and I never have it. So, then the cashier asks me what phone number I put on the application for the card, and I never can remember. At that point, the cashier just hands me a new card—in fact, I bet there are probably fifty versions of me in my supermarket's customer database—and applies the discount to my purchases. The supermarket gives me the discount without any information "payment" whatsoever. Think about that. Is there a digital company on the planet that, when you check out, would give you a discount, or even let you check out for that matter, without an information payment such as your email at the very least? The answer is no.

But GrillCo's situation is worse, because the supermarket knows a *little bit* about me. It just has fifty different records in its customer database labeled "Steve Lucas," one for every one of the loyalty cards it has given me over the years. GrillCo really has no way of knowing that I own one of its grills—and I actually own two! (This is very important to note—sometimes you want to grill with charcoal, but most of the time with natural gas. VERY important. Very.) And it also has no way of knowing, for example, who its brand advocates are—the people like me, who think GrillCo grills are great and who tell everyone they know how happy they are with their purchase. And judging by how successful the company has been, there must be a lot of them.

Now, eventually GrillCo could find its customers, if it were willing to make an effort to do so. If its customers are active on social media, it could, for example, reach out to people who Tweet something great about its products.

Let's play that out. Let's say GrillCo finds Lynne, an accomplished cook who loves her GrillCo grill and raves about it on Twitter, telling everyone who likes to grill they need to buy one. The very next thing that GrillCo should do is create a new profile in its marketing database labeled "Lynnie, Brand Advocate." (Note I said Lynnie, not Lynne. Because an ounce of data cross-matching effort would indicate that Lynne prefers to be called Lynnie, even though a purchase record might indicate otherwise.) It now has Lynnie's name and a way to reach her (through Twitter).

GrillCo could then start searching for the people who follow Lynnie and see what they have to say about GrillCo.

Gathering all that information would allow the marketing team at GrillCo to go from, "I have no idea who this person is" and an unknown IP address, to the beginnings of a digital persona for Lynnie and (hopefully) a social graph of people connected with her that she influences and is influenced by.

The next step for the GrillCo marketing team should be a trip to Facebook to cross-match on Lynnie's Facebook account and identify people who liked what Lynnie had to say. Those that did become part of the digital persona and social graph for Lynnie. GrillCo could then reach out and simply thank Lynnie. It could send her a coupon for a discount on accessories, for example, or simply a note. It doesn't have to be monetary. There are many ways the company could show that it thinks she's important. Here's a personal example of that.

I bought several pairs of Cole Haan shoes online, and a couple of weeks later, I got a note from the company asking if I would mind answering a question from a potential customer who was looking at one of the pairs I had bought. The question was something along the lines of, "How light are these shoes, and do they fit true to size?" Cole Haan could've answered that question, of course. It could've said, "The shoes weigh 6.2 ounces," and added, "Yes, they run true to size."

But it's *always* better if a customer recommends a product to another customer—or potential customer—as opposed to a company opining about how wonderful its products are. Having me weigh in with my opinion allowed Cole Haan to engage me in an extremely powerful way and *also* engage the potential buyer considering its shoes.

Asking me to respond did something else, of course. I said to myself, "Cole Haan thinks enough of me to ask me to go and answer this question for it. I feel valued." Now, Cole Haan was taking a risk, because it didn't know what I was going to say to that potential customer. But the odds are I wouldn't have bought four pairs of its shoes if I didn't like its product. It perceived me correctly as it turns out—as an emerging brand advocate, subsequently even coaxing me to get active and post things on its behalf. Brilliant!

Most companies don't appreciate the unbelievable amount of information about their customers that is out there on the web. If you have an engagement platform, you can build digital profiles or digital personas of these people using all that information.

Most companies don't yet have a system to capture the total amount of digital information available about their customers and prospects (online). If you have an engagement platform, you can build digital profiles or digital personas of your customers, then connect that information to myriad sales and marketing solutions that drive revenue.

An engagement platform is the evolution of something you already have, but probably in just pieces and parts. It's the marketing technology "stack" you've built up in your organization over time, just matured and more integrated. A true engagement platform is a cohesive marketing technology platform that collects all information regarding your customers, prospects, employees, and partners in a central database, then builds personas and profiles of people and accounts based on that captured information. In turn, the engagement platform can orchestrate engagement with individuals and accounts using personalized content from myriad content sources (CMS, etc.). An engagement platform should provide automation, analytics, intelligence, and optimization capabilities across email, social, web, mobile, and, frankly, any other digital channel you use to engage your constituents.

Here's the interesting thing. Cole Haan didn't incent me with, "If you respond to this customer, you'll get a $10 coupon." Simply recognizing me as a good customer was enough to make me feel valued. GrillCo could do the same thing for its high-end customers, the ones who have bought its most expensive products or the ones who've purchased many grills over time.

And if it looked a bit further, GrillCo could find loyal customers who are devoted to its lower-end offerings—like its charcoal grills—and send them an inducement, such as a coupon, to get them to trade up to a more valuable propane-fueled model.

My point is that most companies, especially non-digital natives, do not make this effort to build a robust customer record that contains much more than basic demographic and transaction data—yet they should. Any company—digital native or not—has the ability to build a digital persona of its customers, or a digital profile of its accounts, if it is willing to invest in or build an "engagement platform" that can gather and leverage the kind of information we've been talking about.

Here's a way to think about this. Detailed information about your customers is the equivalent of currency. The leadership team at GrillCo should be contemplating the value of that information and decide what level of short-term monetary gain it might be willing to sacrifice to develop robust digital personas of its customers and prospects. As we have seen, there's a real competitive advantage in doing so.

Companies like GrillCo make the mistake of thinking they are capturing relevant data by asking you to fill out a warranty card, but almost no one does, and so GrillCo doesn't know who bought the grill. As a non-digital native, it has not dawned on GrillCo to offer you something compelling in exchange for you providing your name and email address. It could attach a piece of paper to the front of the grill that says, "Thank you so much for buying our product. We are so happy you did. To show our appreciation, please go to our website, [and they'd provide a link] and we will send you a free spatula and recipe book." The customer would provide their email and physical mailing address, and GrillCo would send out the premiums.

By making this offer, there would be an exchange of value—the customer's name, email, and physical address—in exchange for the premiums—and that reciprocity is important. If you offer something to the customer, they'll consider it fair. Basic horse trading.

Sometimes when I describe how an organization needs to engage this way, the company responds with, "Thank you very much, but we have been around a long time, and while we need to update our business processes, we are not all that eager to change how we engage with our customers."

To which I say, "Your competition may not give you a choice." Let's stay with the GrillCo example. Suppose a competitor comes along and starts selling a grill that comes complete with a subscription so that you never run out of propane.

Here's how it could work. There would be a sensor cap sitting on the propane tank that comes with the grill. When you are low on propane, the sensor would automatically send a signal ordering a refill. Someone would come and haul away your near-empty tank, leaving in its place a completely full one connected to your grill.

If a competitor offered this kind of grill, GrillCo would be in a lot of trouble. Yes, the company has been making very good grills for a very long time. And yes, it has wonderful distribution through the Home Depots and Lowe's of the world, as well as local hardware stores. But it is ripe for disruption.

Why? Because as wonderful as its grills are, people don't buy a GrillCo grill just for the brand. They primarily buy it to produce perfectly grilled steaks, hamburgers, hot dogs, and chicken. It's just like Harvard Business School professor Theodore Levitt wrote years ago: "People don't buy quarter-inch drills. They buy quarter-inch holes."

People are buying GrillCo products to help them produce perfectly grilled food. And GrillCo does a very good job there. But what could stand in the way of producing wonderful food is when your GrillCo grill is running out of propane. When that happens, you have to disconnect the propane tank from the grill, throw the tank in the car, drive to where you can get the tank refilled, wait in line to have it filled, wait in another line to pay, drive back home, and reconnect the tank. And the tank always seems to hit empty when you are having friends or family over—and the place where you get your tank refilled is always closed at that time.

If someone comes along with a grill just about as good as GrillCo's and offers a "never-run-out-of-propane" option, GrillCo could be disrupted. And if GrillCo doesn't believe that it can be disrupted through the Internet of Things (IoT)— in other words, through digital transformation by an upstart offering a simple, Internet-connected cap on a propane tank— it's wrong. It will happen.

And the way that grill company with the "always be ready to cook" service will end up disrupting GrillCo is the same way any digital native would. It will start by monitoring all GrillCo's customers online. Then it will build those digital personas we talked about for every single GrillCo customer on Facebook, on Twitter, and everywhere else they appear online. That's the perfect target market, ripe for the picking.

Why? Because the upstart company will know two things about those people.

1. They like to grill; and

2. They are online.

And then, it will start targeting them with a simple message: "Our grill will deliver perfect food every time. And you will never run out of propane." Maybe it'll call its offering Grilling as a Service (GaaS). (I couldn't resist.)

So, I would tell the GrillCos of the world, "You may not think social listening is strategic, but the company that will put you out of business does!"

The reality is someone ultimately will engage your customer. The question is will it be you? Every month, there is an industry that you were convinced yesterday could not be disrupted by digital transformation . . .

And then it is.

I'm going to paraphrase the CEO of a large enterprise software provider, who says that by the year 2020 there won't be a single company on the planet that will be able to avoid disruption—and that disruption will put many existing companies out of business.

I think he means we need to get our heads out of the sand! Every company is vulnerable.

WHY ENGAGEMENT NEEDS TO BE FRONT AND CENTER IN THE TRANSFORMATION PROCESS

At this point, I think most people will agree that no matter the type of organization, transformation is inevitable. The question then becomes why engagement must be at the heart of your (digital) transformation process.

Marketo's research asked this very question of marketers, and here are the top five answers from B2B customers. They told us if engagement moved front and center it

1. Improved the customer experience overall,

2. Created faster resolution of issues and problems,

3. Built a better relationship with vendors,

4. Allowed them to get the latest information on products and services from the people they bought from, and

5. Resulted in discounts and promotions "tailored to my preferences."

Even with this input, a significant number of people think that transformation is an "inward" thing. Senior managers start by thinking about what needs to change internally, and usually the CEO puts the COO in charge of the change process. She then concentrates on reworking the operations and the business processes. The problem with this approach is that it's the tail wagging the dog. The company proceeds to put new systems and processes in place and *then* tries to engage more effectively with customers. What it *should* do is *engage first* and let customers describe their current and ideal journey—then base digital transformation decisions on that guidance.

You can trace the problems of any business that's struggling, at some level, to failing to listen. You might be saying, "I disagree, most companies fail because they fail to identify new trends or competitors." Fair point, but wouldn't you be more apt to spot disruption if you were constantly engaging your customer base?

The reality is that very few organizations today embrace customer-centric thinking. They say they do, but they don't.

Because they don't take this approach, it is easy to find companies by the thousands that are digitally transforming but are not sure why. They don't have an outcome in mind. They're not measuring how their customers are reacting, so they're not sure if they're going to be able to serve their old customers well. Nor are they certain that they're going to be able to capture new customers efficiently or effectively.

All this uncertainty, to be kind, is not the best way of doing business.

SUMMING UP

If you have an engagement platform, and you are tuned into your customers and learning about their evolving preferences in real time, you will alter the very nature of your company. You will be able to align with the changing wants and needs of your customers.

And this is exactly what customers want you to do. Three out of four B2B customers that Marketo surveyed said, "Brands must have a deep understanding of their needs to engage successfully."

If you have that deep understanding, you will evolve in synchronicity with your customers. Perhaps even ahead of them, which is transformation nirvana! That goes way beyond engaging with people. It goes all the way up to the height of strategy, determining your company's path forward—and leading your customers down a path they don't realize yet that they want to traverse . . . but they will.

The bottom line is if the chief marketing officer (CMO) is effective at listening, learning, and engaging with customers, she should have a more substantial role to play in both the company's product function—what the product group creates and how and for whom—and its strategy.

I can see product and marketing organizations aligning more closely—even merging—because of the real need to understand evolving values and preferences in the Engagement Economy.

We will talk about why this naturally leads us to the conclusion that the CMO needs a new title: CEO (Chief Engagement Officer). That is the subject of chapter 4.

Before we get there, let's spend a couple of minutes making explicit the subtext of these first few chapters: If you want a long-term relationship with customers, engagement needs to be front and center.

That's where we will turn our attention to next.

THREE

Marriage Begins with Engagement

 What you'll learn in this chapter:

- Why engaging with customers is not fluffy stuff.
- How engagement works with (and turbocharges) marketing's traditional 4Ps.
- Why EVERY company is vulnerable without an engagement strategy.
- Why engagement is today's key to creating customers for life.
- Why companies that concentrate on customer engagement generate up to 49% more in revenues than their peers who don't.

Let me begin with a slight disclaimer. Marriage may not be the perfect word for this chapter title. After all, a significant percentage of marriages fail, and no marketer wants to have a failed relationship with a customer or potential customer. That said, the logic underlying the analogy is correct. Every long-term relationship with a customer begins with engagement.

Engagement marketing is no different than the traditional engagement that leads to the altar. Before a couple gets to the point where they are willing to stand before family and friends to say, "I do," they have spent a lot of time getting to know one another. An introduction leads to dates. Or text messages, Snapchat, and a hundred other apps that have replaced "dating." Sigh. Okay, back to the example! Dates lead to long conversations about your hopes and dreams, and those conversations and time together can lead to getting engaged.

If everything in our fictional relationship goes well, then engagement leads to marriage. It is a well-traveled path but one that often takes a long time.[1]

By the same token, virtually no customer relationship begins with marriage. There's the "getting to know one another" phase, which leads to the forming of bonds, then eventually the shopper turns into a buyer, and then, if things go well, a customer for life, and, finally, (we hope) a brand advocate! (If by chance "romance marketing" emerges as a buzzword, I want some credit for the term.)

Now, let me stop right here to make an important point. I am not arguing that engagement is the only thing you have to do to be successful in marketing. You need that empathy we discussed in chapter 2. You need the many metrics we rely on today, like understanding customer acquisition cost, return on marketing investment, and many more. That said, if you make a terrible product, provide awful service, or fail in some other fundamental way to care about your customer, no amount of engagement, or other marketing approach, can save you. In fact, engagement will make the situation worse, because your

---

1 Except in the case of my wife and me. We met and were married in less than six months. I know a good thing when I see it! (You'll have to ask her what she saw in me, but we're still married twenty-four years later!)

(formerly) engaged customer is going to feel remarkably disappointed and will probably communicate her displeasure to everyone she can in person, by phone, and on social media. All that is on top of never doing business with you again.

THIS IS NOT FLUFFY STUFF

I want to make a point that I am going to stress throughout this book: Engagement is not some soft, nice-to-have concept. Not only must it be an integral part of your marketing strategy, its benefits *can be easily quantified.*

In fact, they can be quantified in many ways across customers and beyond, and that "beyond" is important. After all, when we are talking about engagement, we are not simply discussing how to engage customers. We also want to engage prospects and employees.

One of the easiest ways to quantify engagement is through satisfaction and commitment—and both of those things can be measured, of course. Engaged customers are satisfied and committed. They do things like use your app for longer periods of time, consume more of your company's content, and visit your website more often.

Engaged employees are satisfied and committed as well. In fact, they are often the best source of brand advocates! If you want an instant, rabid base of brand advocates, engage your employees.

That said, let's begin with customers. If we have satisfied and engaged our customers, it means we are delivering the outcomes they want. It means we are going beyond their basic needs.

Think back to our TOMS example. TOMS is going beyond my basic need for shoes. It's fulfilling my need to *feel* altruistic.

(continued)

No matter how they purchase—whether it's directly from TOMS or in Nordstrom—the person buying the shoe gets a positive rush of endorphins (it's true!), reinforcing the connection with the brand.

An engaged customer gets satisfaction out of the relationship with the brand, and he is the one who is committed to that brand. The converse is also true. Think about what happens if you are not engaged. You're disaffected. You're frustrated. You're uncommitted.

We see this with employees as well. If our colleagues are engaged, they're excited about where they're working. They feel purpose-driven when they get out of bed and go to work. They are more flexible and forgiving of inevitable mistakes their companies make. And, of course, they do a better job for our customers!

What I am saying is that engagement is a necessary part of the entire marketing strategy you craft.

Let's get to the question that is the central point of this chapter: Do you have an engagement strategy? No, not a marketing strategy. An engagement strategy.

If the answer is no, and I suspect it may be for many readers, then it's time to build one. Don't worry. We'll walk you through how to do it a bit later.

Let's assume for a minute that you do have an engagement strategy or that engagement is a fundamental part of your overall plan. You've undoubtedly seen effective engagement boost the productivity and return on marketing investment (ROMI) of all your marketing programs. Engagement closes the loop and impacts pricing, product, promotion, and placement—the 4Ps of marketing that we all learned about in Marketing 101.

But while the 4Ps are part of a marketer's DNA, we may

have lost our way a bit. I fear that the volume metrics we discussed earlier in the book (like the number of impressions we receive) have led us off course. In fact, it's very difficult for a marketer to *prove* that an impression leads to revenue. Engagement *always* leads to revenue, because there's a closed loop. It amplifies everything you do. It gives a customer or potential customer a reason to respond to the 4Ps in a more meaningful way.

The easiest way to prove that is to look at how organizations typically market. Let's look at each of the 4Ps we all think about every day and see why adding engagement is not only a good idea but paramount.

PRICE

Do you think a relationship based solely on price will be a lasting one?

I don't. But to be fair, I am going to try to make the strongest case possible that it can be by using the poster child for selling on price: Walmart.

Walmart has achieved a relationship with people based solely on price at a scale that is unmatched. The company certainly appeals to one large segment of buyers. But

In today's world of value and engagement, price is going to take a beating. Price is always going to be a consideration, but it's going to be progressively less so as we move toward a service-oriented economy.

what happens if you are a Walmart buyer and someone offers a better price on an item? What's your level of commitment to the company then? Zero.

Here's another way to think about this. Ask yourself if the Walmart shopper is engaged by the Walmart brand, or are they drawn to Walmart solely because of the low prices offered (achieved through economies of scale) that cannot be matched?

In today's world of value and engagement, price is going to take a beating. Price is always going to be a consideration, but it's going to be progressively less so as we move toward a service-oriented economy.

The answer, I think, is obvious. The attraction is the price and not the blue sign with the word Walmart out front.

Clearly Walmart's low-price strategy is working for now. The company recorded nearly a half trillion dollars in sales in 2016. ($482.1 billion to be exact.) But let's hypothesize for a minute. Is it possible to imagine a time when Walmart, because of its heavy dependence on its brick-and-mortar stores and its established physical operations, will not be able to compete against Amazon on price? In a word, "Yes." Over time, it is more than possible that Amazon will be able to offer better prices and a more convenient level of service, because it is not burdened by a heavy brick-and-mortar presence.

Granted, Amazon has acquired Whole Foods, but the revenue generated by Whole Foods' brick-and-mortar presence is a rounding error compared to Amazon's total revenue—and many believe the purchase is designed to expedite Amazon's push into providing fresh food overnight.

All that said, here's the fundamental question: Will Amazon ever put Walmart out of business? I think it *could* happen. (Note, I am steering clear of *when*.) You should think about efficiency and scale. The reality is that I go to Walmart because I can have a low-priced shopping experience. But in the future, I will be able to put on a virtual reality headset and never visit the store. (Or hopefully just use my iPad so I don't look silly.) I will peruse virtual aisles from the comfort of my couch, or in a less Jetson-esque scenario, I'll just click through things online or press a bunch of Amazon Dash buttons. (An Amazon Dash button is an IoT-enabled device that you stick on a wall or cabinet, and with a single press of a button, a specific product like Bounty paper towels is ordered and shipped.)

As long as I know that I'm getting the lowest prices from the retailers I am shopping, I have zero reason to be loyal to Walmart. It just so happens that today people can't compete with Walmart based on price. If Amazon were to change the Dash button to always order the product at the lowest price through a vendor in its network that offers Prime Shipping, why would you ever drive to the store to buy paper towels?

Consider Walmart's slogan: "Low prices every day—guaranteed." What happens when that's no longer sustainable? How will it be able to maintain low prices when Amazon (without the same brick-and-mortar burden) offers better prices and a better experience?

Let's think about where Amazon is headed. Amazon is driving toward a same-day delivery experience for all the goods that you need in your life. It already got it down to two days with Amazon Prime. Soon enough, you'll visit Amazon.com, do all your shopping, click Go, and everything you ordered will show up at your house the same day. Perishable items as well. (That's where Whole Foods comes in.) And since it doesn't have to maintain stores, Amazon will be able to do it at a lower price than Walmart. When that day comes, the whole "lowest prices every day guaranteed" thing goes away.

What happens to Walmart then?

I understand discussing Walmart going out of business is hyperbolic, but is what I just laid out really an impossible scenario? What about your business? If you haven't taken the time to game out scenarios where a nimbler competitor could drive you out of business and how, then you should.

The whole point about engagement is that if your organization's value proposition is largely dependent on one value point—such as "everyday low prices"—then you're a dead man walking. It's just too easy for you to be disrupted.

Everyone—Walmart included—needs to recognize that things change. In Walmart's case, all those brick-and-mortar stores that made it successful might become an albatross around its neck. When that happens, it is going to need more than everyday low prices to succeed.

PRICE VERSUS VALUE

Engagement is the vehicle to drive you from a price-oriented proposition to a value-oriented one. As you make that transition, you'll find yourself engaging with your customers at a deeper level.

Why do some B2B companies use McKinsey when it comes to recommending a strategy for IT outsourcing, instead of contracting with a company in India or China to do it? McKinsey is never going to "win" based on price. That's not its job. Its job is not to be the cheapest. Its job is to be the most informed, the most valuable, the most relevant, and the most aligned to your organization's values when it comes to strategy.

There are plenty of strategy consulting firms that don't care about aligning to your values, and there are plenty of companies that hire those firms that don't care if they do align to values. (They just want to hire the cheapest firm.)

My point is that there's always going to be a contrast between the price player and the value player, but in my mind, engagement is implicit in value. If you say your offering is predicated on value, then you must, by that rationale, provide a deeper level of engagement, be it through customer service, experience, or something else.

Contrast Walmart to Costco. Costco also competes on price, but it has a second dimension that I think goes beyond Walmart's model—engagement. Have you ever walked out of a Costco without seeing the list of services it offers—home heating and air conditioning? Its Vacation Club? Life insurance? The list goes on and on. It is engaging with its customers on multiple levels, well beyond the price of its products. (No, Walmart hosting a McDonald's inside its stores is not engagement.)

The easiest way to describe this is that Costco has added a level of convenience and trust. Convenience in that it offers multiple services in one place. And it implicitly increases buyer trust by putting all those additional services, ergo its "stamp of approval," literally under one roof. It is saying, "If we are offering these things, you can trust us that they will live up to Costco standards."

PRODUCT

Can you compete solely on product? Could you offer a heavily curated line of goods or dedicated services that differentiate your company from the competition? In other words, can you compete by offering unique products or services? I know you think the answer is yes. But my question is do you think it's sustainable in today's world?

Let's play it out. Offering a heavily curated offering is what specialty retailers do. Their premise is that a brand, or a limited number of brands, and (implicitly) differentiated positioning will sustain them. But will it sustain them without engagement? No.

No company, over the long term, can compete on offering unique products without engagement. If it tries, someone else can offer the same product or extremely similar products. If that someone else bundles those products with a better price, superior service, or by appealing to someone's values, you will be in trouble.

You can see how this works if you look at successful specialty retailers. Yes, Tiffany offers specialized products—high-end jewelry and accessories—but it combines it with superior service. Golf Galaxy offers seemingly every golf-related product, but it combines that with a knowledgeable sales staff that can make suggestions that could improve your game.

PROMOTION

When it is done well, engagement is integral to promotion. After all, promotion starts with really understanding your buyers' value drivers. For example, is your buyer risk averse and concerned that something could go wrong with the purchase?

Why do people choose consulting companies like Accenture for a big technology implementation project? Because, generally speaking, no one gets fired for choosing Accenture for this kind of work, even if things don't go as expected. For a risk-averse buyer, Accenture's reputation is vitally important. You need to know that and engage around that point.

On a personal level, here's what I find fascinating. Not a day goes by that I don't receive hundreds of emails offering me a discount on some product or service. It could be low-cost offshore developers offering to help Marketo build software or a T-shirt promotion from Gap. Discounts are not a value driver for me. However, doing something special for my wife on her birthday or our wedding anniversary *is* highly valuable.

What absolutely fascinates me is that not one retailer on the planet has figured out that I am in a serious buying mood one week before either of those dates. I'm not only ready to buy, I am going to buy. And yet, no one has made the effort to look at my social graph, discover my wife on Facebook or Twitter, and simply make the connection! For any retailer reading this book, consider this an open invitation to send me promotions tied to either of those dates! Our anniversary is in May and her birthday is in October. (I've been married long enough not to tell you the year she was born.)

PLACEMENT

Placement needs to be thought of in terms of both a physical and digital context. When the 4Ps were first articulated back in the 1960s, placement meant where you would sell your product and where it would be placed on the store shelf. That's it. Many marketers still concentrate on those points.

We don't think about placement in a digital context as much as we should. An email offer is *absolutely* placement in a digital sense—and it may be completely the wrong place to put your product or message. Social is placement. Mobile is placement. In-app is placement. Website is placement. Partner pages are placement. And yes, ads are placement.

The reality is that digital channels are the brick-and-mortar equivalent of shelves and just as important, if not more so, than physical ones. We know that intuitively, but we need to think about digital placement holistically.

In a B2B context, a marketer needs to know how trends like "consensus" purchasing will affect their sales cycles, how many buyers are involved in the purchase or the decision, who they are, and where each of those people are most likely to be engaged. (A consensus purchase is a B2B decision process where more than one, in fact many, stakeholders in a company work together to make a group-based recommendation and decision.) Technology (and process) such as account-based marketing (ABM) is specifically built to address consensus-purchasing behavior in B2B. (ABM, which is both a methodology/process and technology, is a strategic approach to business marketing based on *account awareness.*)

In scenarios like a consensus purchase, it may be that thirty people with different levels of authority are involved, and each of them might require different kinds of placement. Some will require ads. Some social media. Others mobile or email. The content will vary. But we need to

1. Understand the type of content each player in a consensus purchase will find engaging,

2. Map specific promotions or incentives that will most likely drive response, and

3. Target those players with specific messages based on their digital personas.

Yes, doing all this is more difficult than what we typically do, and the impact is even harder to track given the multitouch attributions. But it's what engagement marketing is all about. It is about being precise versus imprecise across dozens of people and dimensions. And if you choose to be precise versus imprecise, you will win more often than you lose. That's the bottom line.

My takeaway on this? Placement needs to be contemplated in a broader context than it is now for most marketers.

On the physical front, proving impact can be difficult for a number of reasons, including privacy (more on that later), but the reality is that the reason people build apps is in large part to understand placement of their product or service. The stated reason for a retailer to provide you an app might be to make it easier for you to find a nearby location. The ulterior motive is to understand where you go and to optimally place the products you are predisposed to purchase nearby.

Understanding the digital (and physical) traffic patterns of your customer base, where it goes, and why it goes there is a good thing—assuming that you can get that information in an ethical and transparent manner.

I believe marketers can be more upfront and transparent with their customer base. Instead of a rather sterile location tracking statement like "Would you allow me to track your location?" you can share why you'd like someone's location. "We want to track your location so we can serve you better. We'd like to use your location for the sole purpose of placing our product or service closer to where you are to make it more convenient for you. Is that okay with you?" If you take that approach, I think that you'll get more opt-ins than opt-outs.

ARE YOU ENGAGED?

Let's see at this point if you can answer the following questions:

1. How many customer advocates or brand advocates do you have?

2. Who are they?

3. Where are they?

4. How are they promoting your product and to whom?

Can you answer these questions right now off the top of your head? If you can't, then you are *not* driving engagement.

By the way, if you can't answer these questions, you are not alone. Fewer than 5% of marketers can.

BEYOND THE 4PS OF MARKETING: CUSTOMER SERVICE & SUCCESS

Quick question: Do you look at customer service (or success depending on your definition) as a cost center or an engagement opportunity?

Most executives view customer service as an expense. Their position: "It is a cost of doing business. It is the consequence of selling a good or a service. It's just something that we have to do." They don't look at it as an opportunity for engagement. Granted, most companies today are buzzword-compliant and talk about how "customer obsession" or "customer success" is the hallmark of their brand. But you can see that's not true by looking at an organization's investment in customer service and success as a percent of revenue. (More on that later.)

Organizations that carry a cost-centric point of view relative to customer service or success don't understand that their customer service operation gives them access to unprecedented amounts of data—and customers. Not only do you get to capture their name, address, time, issue, email, etc., but you also have a chance to engage with them. Why did they buy your product? What do they like about it? What don't they like? What do they wish you would offer?

Is your service center even capturing that level of data? You don't have to ask *all* these questions on a customer service call or a customer success visit. But making the attempt to gather this intelligence from your customers over time will give you levels of insight your competition just doesn't have.

In addition, the interaction is a relatively easy way to turn a negative into a positive. Let's say a product you use breaks, and you call the customer service number to arrange for a repair. During that call, the organization has the opportunity to turn your potential negative rant into the world's most positive rave. Yes, you've got a broken product (or down service), but if the company can resolve the problem quickly to your satisfaction, it will have a very happy customer. Again, empathy can go a long way toward making that happen.

As Penny Wilson, CMO of Hootsuite, a platform for measuring social media, points out, social media in all forms provides a "unique opportunity to learn who your customers are and what they want. With social data, you can see the unvarnished truth at scale, enabling you to determine what to share with your customers and how to engage with them. And like any personal relationship, it starts with listening. Organizations need to empower their employees to engage with customers and work together in social harmony."

What I find fascinating is how few companies finish a service call with "If you are happy with us, please share your experience at #CompanyNameAwesome." Seriously, why not?

If you are a marketer, no doubt you are thinking, "That's not my department." But if you've been paying close attention to what this book is all about, you should absolutely look at that as *your* job!

Does your company have an engagement initiative where you analyze customer support data that you collect for the specific purpose of identifying opportunities to engage? If not, why not? Customer support or service calls are a massively untapped source for revenue growth when engagement is woven throughout the process.

PeopleMetrics put out a survey a while ago that found companies that focus on customer engagement generate 13% higher revenues on average than their peers. It also said that companies with "poor" customer engagement pay a 36% revenue penalty.

Think about that. You really have this incredibly distorted bell curve in that scenario. Organizations with a focus on customer engagement, literally, have a performance delta of nearly 50% versus those that don't! That's like the customer engagement revenue canyon. That's ridiculous. And awesome. And motivating!

The moral could not be clearer: Companies that make sure their customers are heard benefit.

GETTING THE RELATIONSHIP OFF ON THE RIGHT FOOT

Now, back to dating.

I've been married for twenty-four years, so admittedly the whole dating thing gets fuzzier every year, but from what I recall, if you want a relationship to last, you need to be honest upfront. That is absolutely the same in commerce. You should be clear about what your business does and *what it does not do* and make sure both you and your potential customer understand this from the very beginning.

There are so many times where we want to sell something so badly that we compromise or fudge the truth. I get it. Sales is about never saying no, but I also come from the school of thought that believes profitable relationships are founded on truth.

Here's a great case in point. I just went through a negotiation with a large technology company that was looking to purchase Marketo for its marketing automation platform. The buyers wanted unlimited use of our products for the next three years but told me they would only spend x dollars per year, and x was about 90% less than what an "unlimited" license to our product would normally garner. When I pointed that out, they said, "You'll just have to make up the loss somewhere else, because we're a brand name company that will help you get more customers." (Ever been there before?)

That's a tough spot to be in for any organization, because we as marketers LOVE big brand names! That said, after some contemplation, I elected to respond with, "First of all, I respect your company immensely. We hold a lot of core beliefs and values in common, including investing in local communities, fighting income inequality, and the like. With that said, there's no way we can accept your offer."

I added, "The minimum for us to make money on this transaction is x dollars per year, and let me explain how we calculate that." I then walked them through all the resource and investment that goes into the product we produce, and how we would support and service them as a customer. Then I said, "You don't want me to take your business for less than our absolute minimum price, because if I do, there is no way that I can ensure your success, educate your organization, and properly service your account. I can't provide you a dedicated customer engagement manager or support your growing infrastructure needs." In other words, at the price the buyers wanted to pay, they would fail.

Blunt, yes. But honest, nonetheless.

I went on explaining what the shortfall would be if I accepted their low price, and I concluded by saying, "I can promise, at your requested price, you will have an absolutely terrible engagement and experience. We will both end up resenting each other because of it."

Here's the interesting thing. The buyers signed a three-year agreement with our company above our asking price. The reason I believe they did so was because I was forthright and clear upfront on the level of engagement needed to help them achieve their vision.

Ironically, we are fairly good at this in our personal lives. We have a general sense of the type of person we like and with whom we want to be in relationships. The best relationships, the ones that last, are always founded on shared values and engagement.

As a side note, I'm constantly amazed at how organizations fail to understand what a good versus bad relationship looks like for them. The whole purpose of starting your marketing plan by defining an ideal customer profile (ICP), as well as defining which opportunities you will pass on, is so that you end up working with organizations that your company can properly, profitably, and successfully engage.

We all know this. And we also know that once we deviate from our ICP, engagement starts to go bad.

What this means is that as a B2B marketer, you should invest a disproportionate amount of time defining your ICP. What do your ideal accounts look like? In what industries can we find those organizations? What does their IT department look like? What does their marketing department look like? How many employees do they have? Are they high growth?

The point is that you should decide on how many dimensions your ICP should have, define those dimensions, then qualify *out* every account not on the list. You may be thinking this is nothing more than a named account list, but you would be wrong. A named account list has very few dimensions and shifts very little year to year. An ICP is something entirely different.

When you pursue activities like ICP definition, you'll whittle down your addressable customer base from 50,000 or 60,000 companies to something much smaller. Frankly, an ICP-based subset of your total addressable market (TAM) is all you *should* pursue. At Marketo, we have a very granular ICP, and we even go as far as lower commission rates for account executives who sign clients outside our ICP vs. inside.

Here's an idea to consider. While you can sell to anyone, why not pay your account executives 1.2x your commission rate inside ICP, and for revenue outside the ICP base, pay 0.8x. In other words, disincent them from selling to customers who don't fit your ideal profile.

When we adopted an ICP approach at Marketo, we reduced the number of transactions we handled by 20%, but within nine months, we had doubled the value of our average transaction. This implies we are signing fewer clients than before, but each client is more valuable. The subtext of this is something *very* important. Because we are handling fewer transactions, we can provide more care to each customer. In other words, we can engage more, care more, and know more about each of our customers. Engagement really does drive value.

What this shows is that in B2B marketing, coupling an ICP with better engagement is not just paramount; it will literally make the difference between surviving and thriving.

THE IMPORTANCE OF DEVELOPING AN IDEAL CUSTOMER PROFILE

Why does having an ICP model make for better engagement? Three reasons.

First, you as a company become more self-aware. Too many organizations make the mistake of assuming they can

(continued)

support all enterprise customers equally well. That's a tough assertion to make. The reality is that some companies are just better at enabling mid-sized companies. Some are really good at supporting small "e" enterprise customers. Some are great at supporting massive organizations.

There are fundamental differences among customers. You should know your audience, know your customer, and more importantly, know thyself. This doesn't mean that you shouldn't try to improve in other areas, but it does mean you need to know what you do well today and then focus your organization on your ICPs. And engage!

By doing that, you get to the second advantage. Yes, you may suffer severe anxiety (and a potential blow to your ego) by reducing what you believe to be your total addressable market (TAM). You could easily go from 200,000 TAM companies to just 4,000 companies, but those 4,000 companies are the ones you unequivocally should target. The likelihood of landing one of the 4,000 accounts is multiples higher than landing any of the other 196,000 because of fit. You've heard the expression "square peg in a round hole"? Well your ICP is a round peg for a round hole.

The third advantage is marketing and selling get a heck of a lot easier. You don't have to hype your capabilities or over-promise. You know you are the right solution for the prospect. You can offer pre-built plays by industry and spend less time customizing your message. (That customization, of course, is an economic drag on your company.)

Another best practice in the Engagement Economy is being realistic. In a B2B context, what this means is that you have to determine who sets the customer expectation for your product or service. If, for example, your sales organization is the sole function that sets product and service expectations, I can assure you those expectations will be high, maybe even unachievable. Not because salespeople are bad. Quite the contrary. But they are paid on commission last time I checked. What you can't allow is to promise to your customer that you will deliver a unicorn. Post purchase, when your implementation or services team show up *without* glitter and a fancy horn on its head, then it turns out you are just a racehorse. And there's that awkward expectation re-alignment that often needs to take place. My point is that lasting engagement is based on trust and transparency.

This brings us to a related point that can be made with a question: Why do buyers self-educate today? Because they *don't* fully trust your marketing or salespeople. They are, minimally, suspect of sales and marketing. They will tell you, "The very last person that I want to get my information from is the person who is paid to tell me everything will always be great."

What needs to happen is a big point of this chapter—marketing and sales need to align. They should collaborate and curate an experience for a prospect. The experience should be consistent throughout the needs of the identification, education, buying, and go-live process. The salesperson's job in this context then becomes restating, validating, and verifying the carefully curated experience that your company has already set up. Marketing and sales alignment can make or break any organization, as you undoubtedly know!

I like the way Justin Schuster, Corporate CMO at Acxiom, a publicly held marketing technology company, put it: "I think about marketing as facilitating the buying process. We think we are doing marketing, but the buyer thinks they are doing research."

By the way, sales and marketing alignment is a "holy grail" of sorts for many organizations. The good news is that there is a convergence going on right now between marketing technology and sales technology, enabling better collaboration. As a marketer, you should look for integrated technologies and platforms that connect the last mile with sales! (We will be talking about this in chapter 9.)

This is all part of the engagement process and ensuring the process is exactly what it should be. That leads me to what we will discuss next: Why the CMO really needs to be the CEO—the Chief Engagement Officer.

FOUR

Why the CMO Needs to Be the CEO (Chief Engagement Officer)

 What you'll learn in this chapter:

- The customer owns the brand. The brand doesn't own the customer.
- Why the Chief Marketing Officer must be the steward of the customers' journey (and what role everyone must play.)
- Why the term customer relationship management (CRM) is not only misleading but also extremely dangerous.
- The 4 things that need to replace the 4 Ps.
- Why "vanity metrics" (and you are probably using a few) are a waste of time.

This chapter title is admittedly a bit misleading, but it's a fair point.

What I will be positing in the pages ahead is this: Both the CEO (Chief Executive Officer) and the CMO must carry the title of Chief Engagement Officer, with each respectively working toward a common set of engagement goals and metrics.

That's the main point, but it was too long for a chapter title.

It's where I think you need to land when it comes to ensuring your organization excels at engagement. Both the CEO and CMO need to sleep, eat, live, and breathe engagement.

But if you were to ask who is the internal engagement champion, the person who should be standing on the hill waving the banner of engagement, my answer is that it should be the CMO.

The notion of who owns engagement can be a hot topic, because in most organizations someone will inevitably say, "I own engagement, because I'm building the app for our customers; therefore, I will engage with the customer most of the time." Someone else will say, "I own engagement, because I'm in sales, and I drive all the direct interactions with clients." Still another person will chime in and say, "I own engagement." You get the idea.

The reality is that if you look across an organization, every department—product, sales, customer success, marketing—and nearly every box on the org chart can provide insight into customers. And each could to some degree rightly claim it ultimately should be in charge of engaging with customers.

That's a commonly shared view. Listen to Stephen Yeo, Panasonic's marketing director for Europe, Middle East, and Africa (EMEA). Today, customers are "engaging with different parts of your organization." Furthermore, he states, "They're engaging with marketing. They're engaging with sales. They're engaging with customer service. They could be engaging with your finance department. But who's looking after that customer experience to make sure that it's all joined up and it's all good? This is something that we now have the opportunity to address."

As Stephen addresses it, I think you'll see that nothing is as valuable as the wealth of different viewpoints that marketing has when it comes to the end-to-end engagement experience. Marketing has the most robust point of view in the organization on the customer, given the amount of data that it either has or can easily access.

Now, to underscore how complicated engagement is and how I think it needs to be handled, instead of using "ownership" I prefer using two different words when it comes to describing who is in charge of engagement.

If you say the CMO is in charge of engagement, then all the people in various departments who deal with customers all the time get upset—and rightly so. It's like you are saying to everyone outside of marketing what they do with and for customers is not important.

But if I ask, "Who at company x is the *steward* of the customer journey?" The answer becomes pretty clear, pretty fast.

And the reason for that is easy to understand. The customer journey for most organizations is, as we have said throughout, highly fractured, non-linear, and crosses websites, mobile apps, third-party apps, and even brick-and-mortar properties. There will be multiple interfaces and channels that influence decision-making. As we have discussed, your customer will interact with you in hundreds of ways, and each of these moments is your opportunity to engage.

Given that, let's reframe our earlier question slightly and ask, "Whose job is it to steward the customer's journey across different dimensions so that we can provide them with a positive experience at every touchpoint?" There can't be any other answer but the CMO. The CMO must steward the customer journey across all engagement channels, everywhere!

Not only that, but the CMO must ultimately be responsible for ensuring the customer can *take the buying journey they want,* because in today's complex world, that journey may take them all over the place. The truth is that customers will bounce between brick-and-mortar, mobile, web, Facebook, Google, Twitter, YouTube, and more, always working toward forming an opinion of you.

Customer relationships today are defined by the customer. The sooner organizations realize that, the better off they will be.

That's the customer journey. It's not a straight line. If you are trying to chart it, you might as well close your eyes and just scribble on a piece of paper, because that's what the real road map for a customer journey looks like nowadays. It's self-guided. It includes multiple touchpoints that go through multiple channels and is far from linear. Furthermore, the journey can start so far out on the fringes of the digital "frontier" (e.g., you have no persona defined for an IP address visiting your site) that it can be hard to reach buyers without digital marketing technology.

Ultimately, someone has to stand out front and wave that banner of stewardship of engagement in a non-linear journey. I think that the best person to do that is the CMO. The CMO is armed with the most data about the customer, the myriad devices a customer or prospect uses, the digital channels these buyers prefer, and what messages are most likely to resonate.

Again, it's not a matter of sales "owning" the customer, or, for that matter, any department or line of business "owning" the customer. And it is certainly not about marketing in general, or the CMO in particular, "owning the customer." In fact, no one "owns" the customer. The notion that you do own the relationship with the customer is what gave rise to the term Customer Relationship Management (CRM) to begin with! That's an outdated notion.

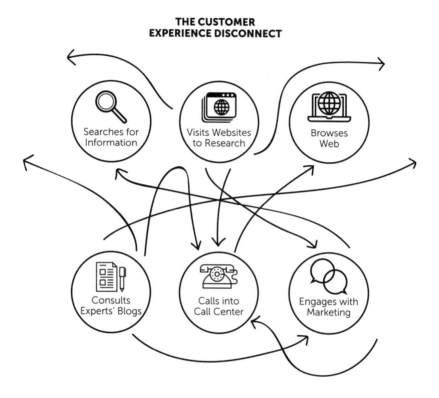

Figure 4.1 The non-linear buyer journey can begin on the fringes of the digital "frontier." Implementing digital marketing technology to reach these fringe locations and unknown buyers is a critical first step toward engagement.

To a certain degree, I even find the acronym CRM grating. The term implies that a vendor believes it can "manage" a customer. I doubt you'll find many customers lining up to be managed, but I can guarantee you that they will line up to be engaged. That's why I like the word "steward." Because, in contrast to the testosterone-laden world of sales, you are not asserting that someone owns the relationship with the customer. A steward is someone who volunteers to care for something throughout its life.

Marketing doesn't own the relationship. But people in marketing in general, and the CMO, do believe that it is our responsibility to steward customers and potential customers through their journey, which will include myriad touchpoints with the organization.

THE CUSTOMER OWNS THE BRAND. THE BRAND DOESN'T OWN THE CUSTOMER.

We need to be careful about the word "ownership" when we talk about our customers. No one owns the relationship with the customer anymore. Anyone who thinks they do is living in a broken mental state. The reality is that the customer is in charge—not the salesperson, not the marketer. What that means is that we are fooling ourselves when there is an internal fight over who owns the customer, because no one does. You are fighting about something that simply doesn't exist.

The customer owns the brand. The brand doesn't own the customer. The customer owns the journey that they want to take on the road to whether or not they want to do business with us.

The concept of CRM, customer relationship management, has been ground into our consciousness for so long that many of us have concluded that this phrase could never change. Well, it has. We need to abandon the notion that managing customers is a desired outcome on the part of the customer. It isn't, and that is why CRM as we know it today

> is dead. If you believe CRM is the bedrock of your customer engagement strategy, it's time to rethink your strategy.
>
> I can't say it more plainly than this: The losing argument is that any one department owns the customer.

What we ultimately want to create is a consistent and relevant customer experience, no matter where the journey begins or the number of touchpoints involved along the way. That is the ideal. As we discussed, the goal is to create a seamless experience for the customer. One of our Marketo B2C users told me that winning a brand advocate is developed over time. That includes delighting the customer at everything from how the package opens to our digital engagement. It's about stitching together all those moments when the customer engages with you so that they feel that the brand is a natural part of their own landscape.

Again, you need someone to supervise and coordinate all this. Having the CMO do it just makes the most sense.

WHY NOT THE CHIEF EXECUTIVE OFFICER?

It's fair to ask if engagement is that important to the organization's success, why isn't the CEO in charge of it? Well, the CEO should be the champion for engagement, but ultimately, the CEO already has a big job to do. I think it's unrealistic given the demands that are put on today's CEO to say that all the CEO's time, 24/7, will be spent stewarding the customer through their journey. I think the CEO has to lead from the front in adopting the mindset of engagement, support the CMO to drive the culture of engagement throughout the organization, and ensure that it happens.

Stated simply, the CEO should be the champion of customer engagement. The CMO should be the steward for the entire company.

WHY YOUR METRICS NEED TO CHANGE

Implicit in our discussion of who should lead the engagement effort is the fact that the very way we market needs to change as well. If you think about the way we have traditionally defined the CMO's job, you'll understand why.

What is a CMO hired to do? The CMO is hired to build brand, drive revenue, and prove return on investment.

If you think about those three things, you realize that for CMOs to keep their jobs, they basically and ultimately must prove their impact. Even CMOs who aren't making an impact will often argue they are. The way ineffective CMOs try to do that is by using data I refer to as "vanity" metrics.

Vanity metrics are numbers that make your marketing efforts look good but really demonstrate very little—if any—positive effect on the business. In other words, vanity metrics really don't move the needle. We need to move from vanity metrics, which have little to no meaning, to engagement metrics, which lead to a stronger, more profitable company.

> If you think you understand customer expectations, wait five minutes.

Let me explain what I am talking about. Let's start with impressions, the most misleading of the vanity metrics, which we touched on in chapter 2. Impressions, as you know, are when a digital ad or any other type of digital media is displayed on a user's screen. It is easy to understand why someone would want to use impressions as a metric. The numbers can get very big, very fast. An ad can easily get *millions, even hundreds of millions,* of impressions if it runs long enough and appears in a number of places.[1]

If you think you understand customer expectations, wait five minutes.

The truth is that millions, hundreds of millions, or even billions of impressions is a meaningless concept. Those numbers don't tell you if any of the people who saw your message actually paid attention to it, and they certainly don't tell you if those people took the action you wanted them to. You may argue that impressions can lead to clicks, clicks lead to visits, etc., etc.—which is all true, but you've ventured into a set of metrics that is extremely difficult to prove.

And even worse, it doesn't reveal if your message in some way alienated even some of the people who saw it. If it did, as we covered before, that will prevent someone from buying from you forever and could very well prompt them to try to keep their friends, families, and (social) followers from buying from you as well.

Obviously, we need something to replace vanity metrics.

Let's divide the discussion of what should replace them into two parts. At the macro level, we'll talk about what we need to do to replace the outdated ways we think about marketing our products and services. Then we will talk about the new metrics we could be using to determine how well we are actually performing relative to engaging our customers.

The goal of both exercises is to move us from vanity metrics to value metrics that have meaning when it comes to engagement.

1　(Please refer to my story in chapter 2 of the marketer playing Six Degrees of Separation and getting one billion impressions. If you are addicted to impression metrics after that story and our discussion here, first seek help, and then please never tell anyone your digital efforts created one billion impressions. You will be perceived as silly—or worse.)

INSTEAD OF THE 4PS

We covered the sacred 4Ps earlier, but the plain fact is we need to replace them if we want our organizations to thrive in the Engagement Economy. We need to go from product to experience. From promotion to advocacy. From price to value, and placement to engagement.

Why? Let's take them one at a time.

We need to go from product to experience because, as we have seen, delivering a good product is not enough. You may have a great product, but if the experience of doing business with you is terrible, customers will eventually find somewhere else to buy.

Here's a simple example. There was absolutely nothing wrong with the compact disc (CD). The music sounded great, and CDs were far easier to play than any product prior. However, you had to buy an entire album even if you only liked one or two songs on the CD. Even though they were, indeed, compact, storage could still be a problem. You *did* have to store them.

REPLACING THE 4PS	
FROM	**TO**
PRODUCT	EXPERIENCE
PROMOTION	ADVOCACY
PRICE	VALUE
PLACEMENT	ENGAGEMENT

Figure 4.2 Maturing our engagement marketing efforts means moving beyond the 4P's we learned about in business school.

When we think about our experience with music today—on demand, streaming, high digital quality, etc.—it seems laughable that we used to carry CDs around in the first place!

The point is that while CDs were a great product, there really wasn't an experience associated with them in contrast to something like Spotify or Pandora. (Even iTunes now seems a bit antiquated, no?)

In fact, the line between product and experience is blurring and, for many products, has disappeared. Is Uber's product the app? Yes. Is Uber's product the network of vehicles and drivers it has amassed? Yes. Is Uber's marketing the app as well? Yes! But I would argue that Uber's product is actually the experience itself, *because* it is the network of cars. (The drivers who are available on demand, 24/7.) It's the variable pricing and the fact that you can track the exact route your driver is taking to pick you up. It is all those things, which in concert create a great experience. When I use Uber, I feel engaged.

In Uber's case, the product is the experience, and the experience is the product.

The same sort of reasoning comes into play when we talk about moving from placement to engagement. We worry so much about things like "Where is my digital ad going to appear?" Or, "What area of the grocery store shelf does my product occupy?" Or, "What part of town should I locate my brick-and-mortar store?" Or, "How close to the 50-yard line is our ad in the football stadium?"

But answer me this: Which of the following is a more powerful engagement? Seeing a (hypothetical) ad in a stadium that says, "Use Deloitte" or getting a text from Deloitte when you are at the stadium that says, "Hey, Susan. Thanks for working with us on that last project. Click here, and we'll send a beer to your seat"?

People fret so much about where an ad is placed. It's not like I go to a Denver Broncos game and say, "Wow, I saw a Deloitte sign, so we should use Deloitte." Placing that ad doesn't make any sense at all to me. In fact, every time I see anything similar to that hypothetical ad when I go to watch the Broncos, I'm thinking, here's an opportunity to engage, but it's wasted on an advertisement.

Myriad companies know I am at the game, based on location tracking with my phone or the Tweets I am tweeting. And they could engage with me personally instead of placing a generic ad. (If you don't think companies know where you are based on the apps on your phone, then pick up your phone and select Settings > Privacy > Location Services.)

It's true that sending me a text out of the blue when I am at a Broncos game might be a little creepy. But if I posted pictures of my daughter and me at the game, then obviously it's okay for someone to know I am there, like my Tweet, and even buy me a hot dog!

If you are leveraging social listening technology, then think about the opportunity to engage with me right there. What could be more powerful? It is certainly better—and more effective— than worrying about where a static ad should be placed.

Why we need to shift from promotion to advocacy is simple. Promotion is all about a company telling you how good their products or services are. There is nothing wrong with that, but there isn't a lot of credibility there either. You expect a company to boast about its offerings, whether or not it's justified.

Some companies have taken to using their customers in their marketing materials, and that is good. A message from a satisfied customer carries more credibility than you bragging about yourself.

But with that said, true advocacy starts when instead of asking your customers to do things, your customers volunteer to do them. In other words, they become brand advocates on their own. That's when you know you've shifted from marketing to engaging, and you've achieved true customer advocacy. So obviously, a pivot should take place. You must shift from featuring customers on a billboard singing your praises or asking them to be a reference for you, to a state where customers promote your brand (digitally and physically) because they love doing business with you.

The next thing we need to evolve is moving from price to value. Including price in the "classic" 4Ps is misleading, because it implies that everyone is affected by price, and common sense tells you this is not the case. We tend to forget that not everyone fits neatly on the supply and demand curve. Admittedly there is a continuum, and on one end, there will always be a cohort of buyers who are driven exclusively by price. That's the only thing that motivates them. That group would include the extreme couponers who are looking to get their grocery bill down to zero if they can.

But if you look at international markets like China and India—where you see rapid middle-class expansion—you'll see dramatic shifts from price-driven to value-driven buyers. That is certainly true on the consumer side.

When you go into B2B selling, value should be your **number one driver**. In the world of enterprise software, SAP is the dominant player in enterprise resource planning (ERP) technology, yet it is far from the lowest-cost provider. It is not positioned for the price-sensitive software buyer. It's priced for the person who's looking for value in their transformation process.

DIGGING DEEPER

Now, let's go down a level and see if we can change the very metrics we use to figure out how good a job we are doing. The first thing we should do is move from revenue, the status quo metric, to lifetime value, where we want to go.

The reason is simple. Implicit in using revenue as a metric is the message that you should become transaction-oriented (i.e., maximize your short-term revenue whether it's value or volume). There are at least three problems with that.

First, in the rush to make a sale, you might not take the time to engage with a customer, hurting the relationship over the long term. Yes, even value-based arguments can be rushed.

The second point is the mirror image of the first. If you are not making sufficient money from a transaction, you will be tempted to keep the engagement level low, so that you have more time to search for more profitable customers.

Customer Lifetime Value (CLV or CLTV) and Return on Marketing Investment (ROMI) are critical engagement metrics, but each focuses on your existing customers. An engaging brand should measure things with their prospective customers in mind as well. After all, don't we also want to provide value to the people we want to become our customers?

The third reason is that in the world I live in—and the world many companies are moving to—all our revenue is recurring. It's entirely subscription based. This is the model that most goods and services will be based on moving forward. In this new world, shareholders *must* consider lifetime value as the priority, because the ultimate goal is to get a relationship, ergo a subscription, to last forever. Furthermore, better customer engagement also positively impacts the five-headed dragon of subscription models: churn rate (churn), monthly recurring revenue (MRR), average revenue per user (ARPU), customer acquisition cost (CAC), and the aforementioned customer lifetime value (CLTV).

Of course, while metrics like CLTV are undoubtedly the right long-term value creation indicators, most publicly traded organizations still operate on a ninety-day life cycle. For them, it's all about driving profitability in the current quarter. But if you truly focus on lifetime value, and you are choosing enough valuable transactions—customers who can buy a lot from you—the business almost becomes self-sustaining.

Next, we need to move from impressions to advocates. As we talked about earlier, most marketers myopically focus on talking big numbers when it comes to impressions. Here's a fundamental question, and, given the amount of discourse we've had in this book on the topic, I think you'll say I am leading the witness here. Would you rather generate one million impressions where you have no visibility into them (i.e., you have no idea if they are leading to higher revenues or even engagement), or would you rather have 10,000 known customer advocates? Okay, that's too easy. How about this: Suppose I said you can have *fifteen* million impressions or just 1,000 customer advocates? I'm betting you'd still choose the advocates, because the amplification of your message over time will FAR surpass fifteen million impressions.

Why? We simply don't know the economic value of an impression. So, we don't know if *more* impressions is better. (Maybe it is, maybe it isn't, but I have yet to be won over by a marketer when they tell me most of their impressions in a campaign are always positive.) However, we know the inherent value of a customer advocate. We know that a customer advocates out there, marketing for us, for free. We can track their

Engage to Win

activity, who they connect with, the prospects they refer, and the like.

CREATING NEW METRICS	
FROM	**TO**
REVENUE	LIFETIME VALUE
LEAD FOCUSED	ACCOUNT FOCUSED
COST PER LEAD	COST PER DEAL
NUMBER OF IMPRESSIONS	NUMBER OF ADVOCATES

Figure 4.3 Just as the 4P's are changing so must the metrics we use to judge our marketing efforts. We need to move from being lead focused to being account focused.

One more point on the topic of lifetime value. I'm seeing some marketers transition from focusing on how many impressions they generate to concentrating on the number of likes they receive on social media. The problem with "likes" is that the number can be manipulated. It takes me all of two seconds to click "like." It doesn't mean I was engaged in any way or even looked at anything in any detail. I just clicked "like." There isn't necessarily any engagement there. Furthermore, likes can be manipulated even further through bots and services where you can literally buy 5,000 "likes" for $10 dollars.

The point is that all these metrics are too easily manipulated and don't give you a real sense for ROMI (return on marketing investment). Nor do they create lifetime value, which IS the point.

A PERFECT EXAMPLE
OF A VANITY METRIC

The next time you go buy a car, think about the buying experience. Is it "amazing"? A perfect 10? I will assume your car buying experience is similar to mine. It takes too long, you are being sold to versus informed, and the dealership is a little too palatial for you to feel like you are getting a good deal.

Once you (finally) complete the paperwork and get the keys, the salesperson will thank you for your business and invariably will say, "You will get a survey in a few days asking you to rate your experience today. My pay is impacted by that rating, so if you could please give us all 10's and 'yesses', that would be great."

Common sense tells you two things.

1. The company you were dealing with is likely to get higher scores than they would have otherwise by simply asking for a good grade. You may not automatically give them one, but a lot of people will be too nice.

2. Those inflated grades don't mean anything.

But even given the flawed data, invariably you are going to see companies who were manipulating their scores to promote their "superior customer service ratings." You know those ads saying "90-something percent of our customers would recommend us to their friends and colleagues." What's worse is that the CEOs of automotive companies make decisions regarding their dealer networks based entirely on manipulated data!

This sort of thing is a *perfect* example of a vanity metric.

If you put a survey out and then tell people to give you a 10, you really don't want to know the truth. That's just self-promotion (and job preservation).

Now, on to shifting from a lead-focused model to an account-focused approach. Let's think about what happens in a sales cycle, especially a B2B sales cycle. We try to generate brand and product awareness through a lot of spend—impressions and the like. Those impressions hopefully convert to inbound contacts, then to Marketing Qualified Leads (MQLs), then Sales Accepted Leads (SALs), and then Sales Qualified Leads (SQLs). FINALLY, a LEAD! Once we have a lead, we allocate even more money to go out and touch the prospect directly or through a partner, hopefully demonstrating value related to our product or service. Finally, we try to expose the prospect to our carefully selected list of references in an attempt to close the deal.

Does this model seem just a little tired?

Besides, as we discussed earlier in the book, consensus purchasing is the driving force in decision-making for B2B organizations.

Let's take the straightforward process of buying a car to explore what a consensus purchase looks like. If you are single, and you have money or decent credit, you're the decision maker. That is not a consensus purchase. However, if you're married, you may not be the sole buyer. (Let's be honest, you aren't.) Purchasing a car in a household is most definitely a consensus purchase.

Just consider the conversation in my house when I said I wanted to buy a new Tesla. My daughter (aka the Chief Information Officer) said I "would look like a nerd driving one." My son (the Chief Technology Officer) told me he loved the idea, but I should get the Model S, not the Model X, because the Model X looks like "a spaceship." My wife (the Chief Executive Officer) said, "Steven, you are a fast car guy. You've always loved big engines and cars that make a lot of noise. Why don't you go look at some other fast cars first before making up your mind?" That, my friends, is Consensus Purchase 101 in the Lucas house, and it's not that different at work.

Model S it is.

Now, let's take on a hypothetical example where a massive organization like the Ford Motor Company decides, for example, "We need to acquire an ERP system." In that decision scenario, there will *never* be one buyer. In fact, there are considerably more than a handful of people to engage like there were in my Tesla example. In the Ford example, there are probably one hundred "buyers." There is no way we can possibly find each one.

This is where account-based engagement becomes even more important. As I explained previously, account-based marketing (ABM) is both a methodology/process and a technological and strategic approach to business marketing based on *account awareness*. You treat and communicate with all members of the account as one.

WE NEED TO MOVE FROM LEAD FOCUS TO ACCOUNT FOCUS

The concept of "the buyer" is dead.

There is no such thing as "the buyer" in B2B marketing. Whether it's inbound marketing, outbound marketing, or even some notable selling methodologies that were at one point all the rage like "customer-centric selling," they all assumed there was one buyer. That is no longer true.

Think about everything we were taught to ask ourselves, like "Who's the technical buyer?" or "Who's the emotional buyer?" All those things you learned in Sales and Marketing 101 are effectively dead. Why? Because there is no such

(continued)

thing as one buyer. Not even if you are dealing directly with the CEO of a company.

What that means is—especially in B2B buying—that we've got to move away from "I have a lead, here is the buyer, call that person," to an account focus where we are asking how we are engaging the entire account.

What naturally follows from that is we need to change the metrics we use from cost per lead to cost per transaction to really reflect how sales works today.

The simplest way to think about ABM is this: You need to influence dozens, sometimes hundreds, of people to get an organization to buy your product or service. Some of those people will speak directly with your account executives. Some will speak with your competitors. Others will only gather digital information online. You may meet some and never meet others, but you must have a technology platform in place that influences each member of the consensus-buying process across web, social, mobile, ads, and every other possible channel. The good news is there are a plethora of ABM technology solutions to automate much of what I am about to share with you. (Full disclosure: Marketo offers one of them.)

Think about all the different dimensions you'll need to consider in an account-based marketing or ABM-selling scenario. You need to:

1. Know the prospect company, its financial performance and priorities.

2. Understand the key trends and economics in its industry.

3. Analyze the prospect's core competitors and their activity.

4. Identify every single person in the company who can influence the decision-making process.

5. Know the digital personas of the individuals at your target prospect, their preferences, values, and goals.

6. Analyze the social intelligence and graph data to understand what matters to everyone involved in the purchasing decision.

7. Comprehend how these people interact with each other and the hierarchy within the group.

8. Determine who in the group is the alpha buyer.

9. Know what digital interactions each person from your target account has undertaken relative to your company—from browsing your website to consuming white papers, attending webinars, and much, much more.

10. Constantly update the people entering and exiting the consensus-buying process. (People leave and join companies all the time, and the dynamics change as a result. Your account executives need to be told.)

11. Buy contact data and webinar/content consumption data from third parties to enrich your ABM point of view.

Sounds like a lot of work, yes? The more important thing is to automatically collect as much of this activity and information as possible. That's why a marketing automation platform with ABM capabilities is so paramount.

Once you've collected all that information, the question is what you do with it. I would suggest the following is a great place to focus your ABM efforts:

1. Develop prospect-specific offers. Include content, landing pages, email, ads, and social engagement relevant to your prospect.

2. Design sales offers to entice your prospect to meet with you. These can surface anywhere—ads, for example—but they should speak to what you know from your ABM data gathering.

3. Personalize, personalize, personalize! You must deliver a personal experience for each different buyer based on the digital persona you've developed. Your website should never look the same to two people from the same account if you have mastered digital persona creation and content delivery to those personas.

4. Build your sales territories around the intelligence you've gathered from ABM monitoring and reporting. This gets back to the ICP concept. Should you include ABM intelligence in ICP definition? Yes!

5. Test. You need to understand how people respond to the plan you build out. Are executives more or less engaged based on the content you pushed?

6. Create a one-to-one executive digital campaign. Engage, engage, engage with execs.

7. You may not have the bandwidth to do everything that I've outlined here, but starting an ABM plan just for executives involved in the purchasing decision is a brilliant starting point.

HAVING THEM COME TO YOU:
THE BRILLIANCE OF BRAND ADVOCATES

As we said, the question to ask with ABM is not how you engage one person, but how do you engage the account? Marketers need to sit down and figure out where the potential buyers are and then determine ways to make sure they can find each and every one so they can engage with them. That requires a lot of work, and it simply may not be possible given the number of people involved in the purchasing decision.

That's why it's always better if prospective customers find you. The best way for them to find you is *not* through an impression or an ad. It is through your advocate. It is by them hearing someone in their industry they know of or respect raving about your product or service.

If you have brand advocates, you can skip over all the hard parts of the sales cycle, because your prospects are being referred to you by your customers. It's a beautiful thing.

Think about what happens in your personal life. If you are going to remodel your kitchen and a friend tells you about this amazing contractor she used, how many times are you going to conduct an exhaustive review of that contractor's references? Rarely. You trust your very positively picky friend. That is the power of the advocate.

WHILE YOU'RE ENGAGING

One of the reasons you want to engage with your customers is to learn what they want. As you have that discussion with them, be careful to distinguish between feedback and ideas. You want ideas.

(continued)

If a customer tells you, "I had a good experience with your company," or they say, "I had a bad one," that is certainly interesting, and it is feedback, but there is nothing you can do with either statement.

Ideas involve something different. Here's how you can help your customers generate ideas for you.

If you're running a hotel chain, instead of asking your customers, "Did you enjoy your stay?" when someone checks out, try sending a personalized email that says, "Thank you for choosing us. We'd like to know what we could improve when it comes to in-room dining, the amenities we offer, and our rooms themselves. What suggestions do you have in these three areas?"

When you do that, and if you put their ideas into effect, you've created an engaged community and an engagement life cycle. We'll talk about that later in the book, but an engagement life cycle is a closed loop that *continually* can drive your company to new heights.

In the world of B2B marketing, you should be looking to identify where your engagement is strong and where it is weak. For example, ask your customer, "If we could make one change in terms of how we market our products or services, what would that be?" or "If we could improve how we engage with your account both digitally and in person, what would you suggest?"

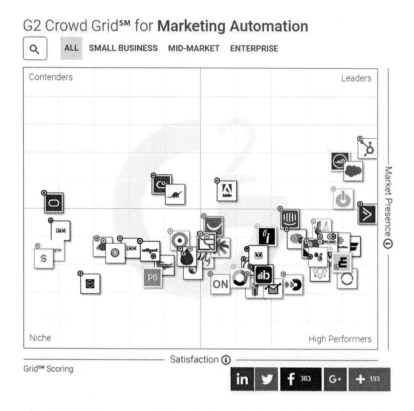

Figure 4.4 In B2B, you can search through ratings and review sites like G2Crowd (above) and TrustRadius to see how customers rate the products they use.

ENGAGEMENT PROCESS

At this point in the book, we're going to get more prescriptive. To that end, it's worth spending a minute talking about how the engagement process works.

Picture a series of concentric rings like the ones in figure 4.5. At the furthest ring you have "discover," where the potential buyer is learning about the product or service you have to offer. This is what I referred to earlier as the digital "frontier." If marketing were a solar system, these would be interactions that happen outside the orbit of Pluto! (Ridiculously far away from Earth.) The question is how do you begin to engage the person who is at this point?

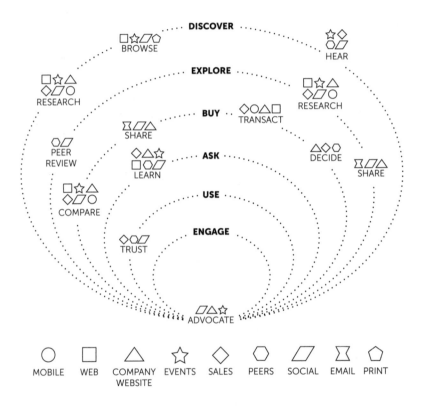

Figure 4.5 Here you see how Forrester Research maps the buyer journey in a series of concentric rings, along with the myriad experiences the buyer will encounter at each phase.

In a face-to-face environment, people know what to do. You can ask questions and gauge interest. But what do you do on the digital frontier of discovery?

Let's say you are thinking about building out a marketing technology stack to begin to track your buyer's journey.

Here's what *typically* happens.

An unknown prospect lands on your homepage. Today,

most B2B organizations believe that the relevant content for a buyer is the gated white paper. It's "Oh, we've got this white paper, and it answers all of your questions." It may not, but even so, you have to give us some type of information payment to even get the white paper (i.e., to get past the gate). This kind of potential exchange—white paper for information—is generic, and everyone who hits your website is exposed to it, even if the offer is irrelevant.

You've just wasted a valuable opportunity to engage.

Here's what *should* happen.

Your marketing technology should understand at a minimum the company of origin of the person who landed on your website based on a reverse IP lookup. That gives you the ability to start customizing content based on some inferential data. (If, by chance, you've been working hard on your customer and prospect database, you may be able to cross reference the device or IP address to a known entity, further increasing your opportunity to serve up relevant content!)

My point here is that the age of the gated white paper is dying. Why? In the first place, it is not necessarily engagement. There are a huge number of people who just don't like white papers. They're not going to take the time to read them. Today, you may need to provide a video, which by the way, begets the need for a system to manage video content.

But the bigger point is that you need to understand what kind of content potential customers want. Is it video? Is it customer reviews and references? Is it case studies? If you don't have a content management system (CMS) to manage all this, now would be a great time to consider one. Not everyone wants the same type of content. And don't forget, there might be many people on a single buying committee, each interested in different content types and topics.

Finally, once you know your prospective customer's content

preference, you need to deliver that content via the channel they prefer.

What we should do throughout the buyer journey from discovery all the way to initial purchase (and beyond) is invite, invite, invite. Invite the prospective customer to answer a few questions that will reveal something about themselves or their company. Invite the prospect to self-guide by indicating what they are interested in versus forcing them to follow a pre-set hierarchy of clicks. You could even ask the prospect how they would like to discover more about your company through video, documents, or existing customer experiences, for example. Let the prospect self-define the journey.

> Regardless of industry or company size, a successful customer experience is dependent on transparency, innovative tools, internal alignment, and closing the loop with customers.

The key thing is to ask where they would like to go and how they would like to proceed. Regardless of industry or company size, a successful customer experience is dependent on transparency, innovative tools, internal alignment, and closing the loop with customers. Invite them to self-select into a journey. I believe that every stage of the buyer journey should be invitation-oriented. In other words, invite me to go through this journey with you based on what I want.

WHERE WE COME OUT

There needs to be fundamental agreement between the CEO and the CMO that going forward we are not going to lie to ourselves. We're not going to be living the lie of vanity metrics; instead, we are going to start living the truth of engagement metrics.

Then, there must be further agreement that together we will work with the board of directors to educate about engagement metrics and reorient expectations around what success looks like. Remember: It's listening, learning, engaging, raising relative lifetime value, creating customer advocates, and everything else we covered in this chapter.

We are, once again, back to the fundamental question posed by this book: Do we want to market to, or engage with, our customers?

The CMO needs to be the steward to make sure we are focused on the right things.

Long live the CMO!

FIVE

Winning in the Engagement Economy

What you'll learn in this chapter:

- The specific tactics your company needs to employ to make engagement successful.
- What an Engagement Maturity Assessment is and how to conduct one.
- Why a focus on Customer Lifetime Value is more important than ever and what metrics you should use to track it.
- How customers want engagement to work.
- Why leveraging technology is the biggest challenge marketers face.

We have covered a lot of ground fairly quickly in the first few chapters. By now you understand why we must engage to win and how—at a high level—you need to think about engaging with your customers and the people you would like to *be* your customers.

In the second half of the book—which begins now—we are going to turn our attention to *how* you should engage (i.e., what specific tactics your organization needs to employ, and why, to thrive in the Engagement Economy).

Where you start and how long it will take to incorporate totally integrated engagement into your marketing strategy and programs will depend on your organization's current level of engagement maturity. Of course, it also depends on where you are in your digital transformation. (See our discussion in chapter 2.)

But there are three things you can do upfront to make the organizational change easier and more efficient. Let's take them in the order you should employ them.

First is something we call an Engagement Maturity Assessment, which we frequently conduct for our clients at Marketo (see the following box). As part of this, you want to look at key elements like how marketing functions are distributed within your organization and how well they are working.

Let's say you work at Foo Express, a global company with 15,000 employees. (They make Foo.) It would be exceptionally rare for Foo to have a single, centralized marketing function. Odds are, corporate marketing and field marketing operations will be at Foo's headquarters. If Foo is a US-based company doing business overseas, undoubtedly it will also maintain marketing field operations in local geographies for myriad reasons.

So, it's entirely possible that Foo's US-based field marketing operations will be more mature than, say, its field marketing operations in Latin America. Of course, it could be the other way around if Foo were based in Latin America.

ENGAGEMENT MATURITY ASSESSMENT

It is always easier to accomplish a goal if you know exactly how far you are from success and what resources you can bring to the problem. That is what the Engagement Maturity Assessment helps you understand.

It measures how far along your organization is in six key areas.

Engagement Maturity Assessment Model Option 1

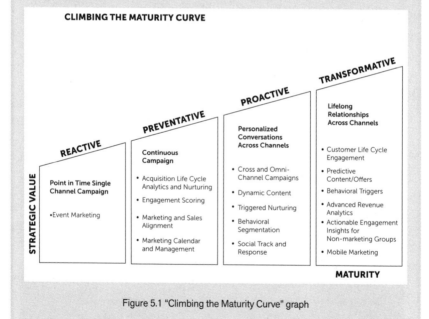

CLIMBING THE MATURITY CURVE

TRANSFORMATIVE

PROACTIVE

PREVENTATIVE

REACTIVE

STRATEGIC VALUE

Point in Time Single Channel Campaign

• Event Marketing

Continuous Campaign

• Acquisition Life Cycle Analytics and Nurturing

• Engagement Scoring

• Marketing and Sales Alignment

• Marketing Calendar and Management

Personalized Conversations Across Channels

• Cross and Omni-Channel Campaigns

• Dynamic Content

• Triggered Nurturing

• Behavioral Segmentation

• Social Track and Response

Lifelong Relationships Across Channels

• Customer Life Cycle Engagement

• Predictive Content/Offers

• Behavioral Triggers

• Advanced Revenue Analytics

• Actionable Engagement Insights for Non-marketing Groups

• Mobile Marketing

MATURITY

Figure 5.1 "Climbing the Maturity Curve" graph

Engagement Maturity Assessment Model 1 does a good job of laying out what you are seeking.

(continued)

Strategy

You want to go from having a strategy that is solely created by reacting to events to one where you are continuously planning for an uncertain future and controlling as much as you can.

Technology

The ultimate goal here is to have a fully integrated marketing platform that works across—and with—all channels.

Execution:

You need to move from one-offs to a global alignment of getting the most important things done.

Customer Journey

As we have talked about, you can't dictate the customer's journey, but you can understand how customers want to interact with you and design your organization to accommodate them.

Optimization

Everything that can be automated is, and that automation is helping you predict the future.

Process

The objective is to move from doing everything ad hoc to making sure the way business is done is not only automated but also drives your business in the right direction.

That brings us to Assessment Model 2, where you see what you are ultimately trying to accomplish: moving from the left side of the graphic to the right.

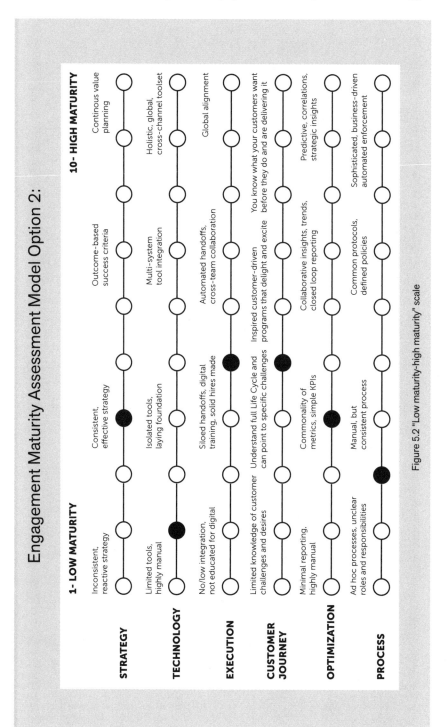

Engagement Maturity Assessment Model Option 2:

1- LOW MATURITY

10- HIGH MATURITY

STRATEGY
Inconsistent, reactive strategy — Consistent, effective strategy — Outcome-based success criteria — Continous value planning

TECHNOLOGY
Limited tools, highly manual — Isolated tools, laying foundation — Multi-system tool integration — Holistic, global, cross-channel toolset

EXECUTION
No/low integration, not educated for digital — Siloed handoffs, digital training, solid hires made — Automated handoffs, cross-team collaboration — Global alignment

CUSTOMER JOURNEY
Limited knowledge of customer challenges and desires — Understand full Life Cycle and can point to specific challenges — Inspired customer-driven programs that delight and excite — You know what your customers want before they do and are delivering it

OPTIMIZATION
Minimal reporting, highly manual — Commonality of metrics, simple KPIs — Collaborative insights, trends, closed loop reporting — Predictive, correlations, strategic insights

PROCESS
Ad hoc processes, unclear roles and responsibilities — Manual, but consistent process — Common protocols, defined policies — Sophisticated, business-driven automated enforcement

Figure 5.2 "Low maturity-high maturity" scale

This doesn't mean that Foo's Latin American operations are necessarily immature. But it does mean that you can't say, "Let's change how we engage with our customers across the board all over the world simultaneously," and expect everyone to immediately "get it," then implement those changes effectively. Assuming consistent levels of maturity and readiness in a marketing organization is a recipe for failure.

Beyond marketing maturity, you also want to know your company's EQ—not emotional quotient, but its *engagement quotient*. This is what I call the engagement strategy life cycle (see previous page). You need to determine how well you engage with your customers. The truth is some organizations are going to be profoundly more engaged with their customers than others, but you have to start somewhere, and starting to engage more is what's critical.

For example, some companies will refuse to use anything except email marketing technology. They like it; it's easy; and hey, why rock the boat? I can assure you that these kinds of marketers will eventually be relegated to the purgatory that is the junk mail filter.

Then you have more mature marketing organizations, ones that will be operating across a range of digital channels—social, mobile, web, mail, ads, and the like. As you move up the maturity curve, some companies may find that the most effective marketing for them is social, and others may find social to be completely useless. The point is that more mature marketing organizations know what works for them so they can engage more efficiently.

In addition to the Engagement Maturity and Engagement Quotient/Strategy assessments, you need one more thing: an extremely comprehensive map of your buyer's journey. The reality is, as we've talked about throughout this book, no buyer journey is linear. We know that. But what does it actually *look* like?

To figure that out, you need to know how they want to interact with you.

As you start to move from strategy to tactics, here are three things you will need:

- An Engagement Maturity Assessment.
- An Engagement Quotient and Strategy Assessment to determine how intelligently your organization engages with its customers.
- A map of how your customers interact with you.

Taking these three steps will make your transformation to engagement marketing far easier. You ask:

- What is our customer's ideal journey in dealing with us?

- How well are we engaging with customers today?

- How far along the path are we in relation to where we want to be?

If you have those three bits of information, you can start to move fairly quickly from yesterday's marketing tactics to the digital science of marketing engagement. As Colin Day, vice president, Global Demand Centre & Marketing CTO for FIS, a Fortune 300 company, says correctly, "The Engagement Economy is really about how you manage the entire relationship and life cycle of the client and prospect, engaging with them in a personalized way from the first time you interact with them through the buying journey, and then post-journey as well."

WHAT WILL CHANGE?

We will be going into all this in detail in later chapters—indeed, the discussions will make up the remainder of the book—but let's foreshadow what's ahead. We'll start with a discussion of how your revenue growth drivers are going to change.

I asserted earlier that your focus will need to shift from a short-term, transaction-oriented approach to concentrating on customer lifetime value. At the end of the day, engagement is not about the quick sale. It is about raising the relative lifetime value of your customer base (while expanding that base as well). So, that's what should start to change first and foremost—understanding how valuable your customers are to you over an extended period of time.

If a CEO, marketer, or other executive is thinking about driving engagement for short-term gain, they should put the book down now. They shouldn't waste their time reading further. While they are focusing exclusively on how to get the next sale, someone is going to form a long-term relationship with their high-value customers, reducing their short-term focused company over time to commodity status or worse.

After the engagement quotient, the second metric you are going to need to pay more attention to is average revenue per user (ARPU). It could also be revenue per account or revenue per customer, but you want to increase this metric on a consistent basis. All the data shows that a more engaged customer buys more over a longer period.

So, revenue drivers need to change.

From there, you need an increased focus on the lifestyle of your customers.

LIFESTYLE

The notion here is simple. The buyer is not a single-dimension individual motivated by a single force. For example, as we talked about before, I think we make very poor assumptions that people are driven solely by price today. The modern buyer is a very complex being. They are influenced by many things—not just price, not just promotion. Remember the two women who purchased TOMS shoes?

That's why in marketing, you should really be focused on the lifestyle of your buyers. I am going to use the term "buyers" in reference to a number of buyers at a specific account from now on—versus referring to individual buyers across all organizations. Why? Because we've introduced the topic of ABM (in chapter 4), and that's exactly where you need to be focused. B2B marketers who do not sleep, eat, and breathe ABM will fail.

Disagree? Consider this: Can you say to the average salesperson, "Hey, I want you to go out and gather as much intel as possible on every human being at the Ford Motor Company who is going to be involved in the purchase of our product or service." Is that realistic? Absolutely not; it's an absurd notion.

However, if you operationalize an engagement platform (i.e., technology) to do it, it's more than possible. You can unleash this system to discover everything that is valuable about decision makers in an account. From that you'll build this ridiculously rich account profile—then you'll inevitably understand more about their professional (and even personal) lifestyles and what will entice them to engage with you.

That brings us to the third thing we need to change: how to think about marketing technology. In chapter 9, we will be talking about how you as a marketer can don the Iron Woman (or Man) suit of Artificial Intelligence and change the game.

SCALE

Ultimately, you'll use an engagement strategy to jump-start your growth, both with existing customers and to attract new ones. This means marketing organizations will have to think about creating different rules for the demand generation team, the people who manage the leads that flow through the company. Just as the buyer journey is non-linear, the reality is the leads and opportunities that flow through your pipeline are going to be non-linear as well. As marketers, we like to focus on volume metrics like cost per lead and conversion rate optimization. I get it. As we push more and more volume through our traditional "funnel," tweaking these can produce measurable benefits, and I encourage that. However, let's go back to a fact I mentioned earlier in passing. There are literally two billion people using Facebook today. That's a lot of people to market to digitally.

So, this is a defining moment for you. Do you keep the marketing model you have in place today, attempting to crank through two billion potential contacts on Facebook (and the billions that aren't), or do you look to drive more value? Here is the real question: How do you intimately engage with two billion people?

The question is more difficult than that, because you don't necessarily want to engage with all two billion people (unless maybe you are Coca-Cola). In the Engagement Economy, we want to find the signal in the noise, the individuals who are worth our time to engage with.

So, how do you find them in a sea of two billion people?

> Integrating and orchestrating the overwhelming number of marketing technology tools available today is the #1 challenge marketers face.

The first thing you need to do is start listening. But here's a silly question. How do you listen to two billion people? The answer is: Without the right technology, you don't. You can't. It just isn't possible.

You should leverage technology to do two things.

First, use it to establish an audience profile via technology, like an audience platform that finds people on social media who match your ideal customer profile (ICP).

And you want to employ that technology to listen closely to your existing customers. What do they like? What do they not like about your offering? What do they talk about frequently?

Then refine, refine, refine.

If you are reading and you're shrugging your shoulders saying, "Well, I tried social listening, but no one's talking about me," think again. It means you have yet to really connect what you've heard with the message you are spreading across the various digital channels you are using. My favorite example of what not to do here is using a social listening product and working very hard to gather information on prospects and then turning around and attempting to engage with those prospects via email. Ugh.

IT ONLY GETS HARDER FROM HERE

That's an attempt at scaling engagement in today's world. The reality is that we are not doing as good a job as we could. Research that Marketo commissioned showed that 82% of marketers believe they have a deep understanding of how customers want to be engaged, yet customers disagree.

- Some 64% of B2B customers (and 69% of B2C ones) think engagements with companies they do business with are relevant but still primarily transactional.

- Only a third of B2B customers and just 16% of B2C customers say that brands take the time to understand them and develop a relationship.

And this disconnect is only likely to grow in the future.

It's already difficult to listen, learn, and engage across the primary social media channels—Facebook, Twitter, and Instagram (and maybe Snapchat if you like an augmented party hat on your head).

Now, let's fast-forward ten years. Six billion plus people on the planet will have an email address. Two-thirds of everyone on Earth will have smartphones. How will you handle this volume and find the opportunity signal in all that noise? You'll need an engagement platform that can listen across all those technologies, all those digital channels, all those broadcast mechanisms, and do all that listening in an unprecedented fashion.

But that is just the starting point. You must then ingest all that listening information and, as we talked about earlier, build personalized digital profiles of each of your customers. And oh, by the way, your engagement system must listen in real time and continually update those digital personas or profiles, since, as you know, customer sentiment can change in five minutes. Plus, that same system has to be able to automatically engage with those same buyers in the channels that they prefer.

So, what does scale really mean? It's listening, learning, and engaging with potentially millions, if not hundreds of millions or even billions, of potential consumers or buyers. It's aggregating that information; learning about the people you are trying to reach based on that data; and then re-engaging them through the channels they prefer.

If that sounds like finding a needle in a haystack, it is. What we are talking about is the marketer getting profoundly better at finding a tiny signal amidst a massive amount of noise. With countless machines and devices in the world of the IoT connecting online, there will be more noise in the coming years. So, you are going to have to get even better at listening and responding, real fast.

> Ten years from now, I firmly believe everyone on Earth will be connected to a single, integrated, global digital network.

Ten years from now, I firmly believe everyone on Earth will be connected to a single, integrated, global digital network. So, engaging at scale means building out and then constantly curating these massive numbers of profiles to find the specific audience you are searching for.

You must take this approach to satisfy your audience. Further Marketo research shows that customers want engagement to be:

- Personalized. As one customer told us: "I will be happier when brands interact with me on a more personal level. When they do, I will be more likely to have a great relationship with them."

- Seamless. Integrating customer information across touchpoints is important to customers, and most don't think we are doing it well.

- Consistent. B2B and B2C customers agree that providing a consistent experience is key to effective engagement. However, only one-third of them think companies are providing that consistent experience.

- Innovative. Customers think that the most effective companies are using innovative forms of engagement, yet very few think the way that they are being engaged today is innovative. Again, we see a disconnect here. Nearly half of marketers (48%) think their customer engagements are "very" or "extremely" innovative, but only 33% of B2B customers and just 23% of B2C customers agree.

In chapter 7, we will discuss in more detail how important technology, specifically an engagement platform, is to the future of marketing.

For now, I'll share one quick story involving Marketo to give you an idea of the sort of things we will be covering.

More than 6,000 people attended the 2017 Marketing Nation® Summit, our annual marketing industry conference. Someone attending tweeted that he didn't feel there was enough practical content at the show. Our automated system of social listening identified this as a negative Tweet.

Two things happened as a result. One, we generated an automatic response that said, and I'm paraphrasing, "Hey, we appreciate your comments about the Marketing Nation. May we contact you to follow up?"

The second thing that happened is that the system routed the original Tweet to my inbox. It automatically identified who should respond to the Tweet and, in this case, that was me.

I reached out and tweeted, "Hey, I appreciate your input. We will definitely include more practical content next year."

The very next Tweet that came from him was, "CEO of Marketo is listening. This makes a huge difference to me."

From there, we will be discussing how your marketing organization and, indeed, your company need to be organized in order to succeed in the Engagement Economy.

During that discussion, we are going to make two major points.

First, *customer experience* is job one when it comes to engagement. Marketers miss this. They think customer experience is their digitally owned channels like web, email, and social media, and earned channels like their ads. The reality is that customer experience should be complete, holistic, 100% connected. It must go beyond digital-owned and earned, into every touchpoint that you have with your brand, or the product, for engagement to be truly successful.

That means it extends from customer support to sales and even includes third-party interactions with the brand. (If you are using suppliers to take care of your customers, or outsourcing part of the work, the organizations that you delegate to need to be as dedicated to taking care of your customers as you are.)

Most marketers really haven't thought about that. Our research showed that only 60% of companies' engagement strategies include their partners.

As we will see in the B2B space, the customer experience is even more important than it is in B2C.

The second point? The structure you adopt will have to be remarkably flexible, to accommodate not only your customers' non-linear interactions with your organization but also the endless innovation that is present today—and that will only accelerate.

With that by way of background, let's talk about how you can get your organization operating most efficiently in the Engagement Economy.

LA CHAPELLE
35 SPITAL SQUARE
LONDON
E1 6DY
THANK YOU

21:57:58   05/04/18

Receipt 0266
MID: *********24968   TID: ****+2268

MASTERCARD
************8256
A0000000041010   CHIP

SALE   £236.42

PIN VERIFIED
APPROVED
AUTH CODE: 030029
E4E71048IF6489FF   TC
S:1

SIX

New Revenue Growth Drivers

What you'll learn in this chapter:

- Two new metrics you need to add to your existing KPIs.
- How fine-tuning your Ideal Customer Profile will make your life dramatically easier.
- Why you need to prepare for subscription-based "everything."
- Why you need a clear engagement model.
- Why brand advocates are critical for success in the Engagement Economy.

Let me be clear upfront in explaining what we will cover in this chapter. I am not suggesting that we forget about the traditional marketing (and general) measures that help describe a healthy, growing company. Metrics such as increasing revenues, expanding margins, gains in market share, high returns on investment, capital and shareholder value, funnel size, conversion rates, etc., all have their place. To be a strong and thriving organization in the Engagement Economy, all those things and more are necessary—but insufficient. You need to incorporate engagement metrics!

Now, there are myriad engagement metrics that marketers use today, things like Time on [web] Site, Engaged Page Views, Content Consumption, and many more. I fully support any metric that further reveals the level of engagement between a buyer and a brand.

All that said, to integrate engagement more fundamentally into your organization's operations, you need to add and manage two critical metrics that can make the difference between winning and losing over the long term. Those metrics are:

1. The lifetime value of your customers (aka CLTV)

2. The number of brand advocates your organization has

The logic behind those two metrics is simple and goes back to the very premise of the book. If value in the Engagement Economy is built on meaningful relationships, then you need ways and means to measure the value of those relationships.

Ergo, taking action to drive CLTV and build your base of advocates can make all the difference. Why?

- If customers are staying with you longer, they are contributing a greater amount to your revenue and earnings.

- If customers are shouting from the rooftops about how much they love your offerings, your reach is dramatically extended.

A customer who stays with you longer and who pays you more over time is just another way of confirming that you are creating long-term customer value. A customer who is declaring openly that they are a fan of your brand and service is a brand advocate. That's why these are the two new measures that matter most.

In the old, acquisition-based marketing world, we were consumed with clicks and impressions. In the Engagement Economy, marketing alignment must span the entire customer journey, not just focus on the sale. This implies that different metrics matter.

Instilling the importance of these two measures and bringing them front and center is going to require some work for most organizations.

The CEO, CMO, chief sales officer, chief revenue officer, and everyone else at a senior level in charge of increasing sales is under pressure to continuously show growth on a quarter-by-quarter basis. This is especially true in publicly-traded organizations.

> In the old, acquisition-based marketing world, we were consumed with clicks and impressions. In the Engagement Economy, marketing alignment must span the entire customer journey, not just focus on the sale. This implies that different metrics matter.

That pressure ultimately translates into more focus on quick hits and short-term gains and less focus on the greater sales and earnings that come from keeping a customer for life. All the attention on the short term can force the CMO and the sales organization back into more tactical activities—the volume and vanity metrics we discussed before. And that takes time away from our new value metrics, which are requisite for success.

Ultimately, the CMO needs to have a conversation about customer lifetime value with the CEO, the head of sales, and everyone else charged with generating revenue. They need to reach alignment on what CLTV means to them, why it matters, and how it will drive long-term success.

Your demand generation team, your corporate marketing team, and your product marketing team—typically the big three pillars of marketing—should also align around the same set of metrics designed to drive long-term value and brand advocacy. This concept is somewhat at odds with the notion of the demand generation team only being measured on Marketing Qualified Leads or MQLs, which have nothing to do with lifetime value or brand advocacy. Likewise, corporate marketing, when measured only on how many events it delivers or site visits are driven, doesn't affect CLTV or advocacy. I like to think about how effective Apple is at keeping its customers loyal, and I can't help but see the trappings of engagement and experience in everything it does!

Beyond agreement that CLTV and advocacy are "important," we need the entire organization to align, top to bottom and end to end around them. Why? Because ultimately those KPIs are the true measure of success for the organization. Some 87% of marketing dollars spent on average today are still spent on customer acquisition, and that has to change. That's the challenge.

Marketers are still being incented primarily to generate leads, as opposed to creating higher level value through engagement. That isn't going to change unless the organization sets new incentives that are aligned company wide. This alignment needs to be in place if you are going to create a successful company going forward. Some of the most valuable companies in the world—Alphabet (Google), Apple, Johnson & Johnson, and Pepsi—run very effective programs oriented around the lifetime value of a customer.

Lifetime value is actually the perfect output of engagement throughout a customer journey. Why? Because it requires you to give the people who do business with you a great experience from the first interaction with your brand all the way to the point they become successful. And that's what you really want: Your customer achieving success because they bought and use your product or service.

Customer success leads to brand advocacy.

TWO TYPES OF ORGANIZATIONS

As I've worked with organizations all over the world, I've encountered two types: those that focus on customer lifetime value and those that don't. The ones that don't generally are less profitable. Why? In large part, it is because their customer base keeps churning, and they have to spend a tremendous amount of money acquiring new customers. That's a vicious cycle that's tough to extract yourself from.

THE FOCUS ON LIFETIME VALUE MAKES SENSE FOR EVERYONE

I sometimes hear pushback about what we have been discussing.

People who hear me explain that organizations need to be focused on lifetime customer value nod their heads in agreement. Then they say I am minimizing an important point by asserting that just about every company, public or not, is under pressure to "make their numbers" (their sales and earnings goals for the next ninety days).

I do understand that. But I see it as a question of what the company is focused on. Is it short-term gain or long-term value and profitability?

As a shareholder of publicly-traded companies, I choose to invest in companies that I believe are not focused solely on

(continued)

the next ninety days. They are focused on long-term share-holder value.

Look at what the best investors in the world do when it comes to picking stocks. Warren Buffett is a great case. If you go through his portfolio and look at his top holdings, which include Coca-Cola, Kraft, Heinz, and other stalwart brands, you'll see that he invests in companies that are focused on long-term shareholder value. And the way you create long-term shareholder value is by taking care of your customers.

Some fascinating research from McKinsey bears this out. I urge you to read it at http://www.mckinsey.com/global-themes/long-term-capitalism/where-companies-with-a-long-term-view-outperform-their-peers. The management consulting firm writes that firms that concentrate on the long term outperform companies that have a short-term perspective by a wide margin.

Over a fifteen-year period (2001–2016) the following held true for these companies:

- Revenues were 47% higher,

- Earnings were 36% greater, and

- Market capitalization was $7 billion more.

I'm not saying that making the quarterly number is not important. But I believe there is a strategy that will allow organizations to grow customer value long term *and* make their numbers as well. Here's the reality: Companies that focus on customer lifetime value have more effectively weathered economic downturns than companies that have not. That's because their customers continue to do business with them in good times and bad. The data supports this over and over again.

Yet I will assert that fewer than 25% of all companies use lifetime value as a key measure their management team looks at on a regular basis. Here's the key takeaway: Customer lifetime value is up there with top-line revenue, profitability, EBITDA, and the like as a key measure.

Frankly, I think shareholders need to be looking at a company's customer lifetime value metric when they are thinking about investing. The McKinsey data shows that this would be a wise course, and some investors have already started to take note. In 2016, S&P launched an index (The S&P Long-Term Value Creation Index) that comprised 250 companies that have taken a long-term focus when it comes to running their business.

AN EASIER WAY TO DO THIS

Creating a customer for life becomes easier if you start by using your Ideal Customer Profile (ICP) to attract the people you want to do business with. It's a question of "fit." We all know that our companies serve certain types and profiles of customers better than others. Take Marketo. In specific industries, our retention rate is double other ones, yet we apply the same amount of resources equally. Why is that the case? Fit.

A little more on this is needed, I think, because you should contemplate this for your own organization. As I stated on "fit," every company I have ever worked with or for has had two types of customers. One type is the customers they serve incredibly well because of the natural disposition and orientation of their company. The other includes customers they don't serve well. But for tactical reasons (i.e., quarterly or short-term gain or a lack of definition or clarity around their ICP) they work with these customers. This situation almost always ends up being less than optimal.

I would defy anyone to show me how a customer who is outside of a company's ICP is more profitable than a customer who fits within the ICP. And by the way, an ideal customer profile is not created by just asking, "What type of company do we make the most money from in what particular industry?" The ideal customer profile, as we discussed previously, addresses who we serve most effectively, their profile within the industry, and the geographies we serve best, among other things. The type of question you need to answer with ICP is: If you're selling a technology (for example), does the company that you're selling to have the capacity to even support your product or service? If not, does your company have the capacity to take on your customer's potential deficits? If the answer is no on both questions, then why take the business from them if you know they will fail? Short-termism.

> Long-term customer value is the ultimate engagement metric.

A little more on my company. At Marketo, our win rate triples when we go after prospects that already have marketing automation software! Seems counterintuitive as there is an incumbent, yet it's true! The lifetime value of those customers is double our average. Why? What we find is that a more educated buyer is more successful using our products.

When it comes to your ideal customer profile, you need to look beyond wins to factors such as profitability. There are so many organizations that don't truly comprehend how ICP affects one of the biggest drivers of profitability—customer acquisition cost (CAC). I guarantee that companies without an ICP or without clarity about their ICP throughout their marketing and sales organizations will have a higher CAC than organizations that do understand their ICP. Those higher costs, of course, reduce profitability.

Again, I understand the pushback, which generally falls into one of two categories:

- By focusing on your ICP, you are missing out on revenues from customers that don't fit the profile (aka "Bluebirds"), and

- By trying to create an ICP you're winnowing the number of targets you're going to go after, increasing the pressure to land each one.

Got it.

My response to those arguments is something I mentioned in the beginning of the book when we discussed the reach one has today through digital means. More to the point, in the digital world in which we live, it is relatively easy to reach an unlimited number of companies. The companies that try to do that and try to reach every conceivable buyer within those organizations take an approach that can best be described as "the blindfold and butterfly net" model. It's where you blindfold all your salespeople and marketers, give them a butterfly net, and say, "Go."

They run around for ninety days at a time swinging the butterfly net, and then at the end of the quarter, they take off the blindfold, and you all get to see what they've caught. Then it's up to the rest of the organization—product, legal, finance, tech—to figure out how to serve this randomly collected group of customers, profitably.

If you decide to market (or sell) in that mode, you are making an incredibly costly choice. In other words, if you don't have a clear, crisp ICP definition or just don't care, just know you are effectively saying, "I'm going to take the more expensive route to grow my company." As my mother used to say, "Ooookaaay for you!"

Ultimately, it makes more sense to focus on the people with the highest propensity to buy, who represent the path of least resistance to you obtaining the sale. There is no guarantee they will become customers, because you may do something to screw things up in the business process. And they may never become customers for life, but they give you the greatest chance.

SUBSCRIPTIONS

Focusing on the long-term value of the customer relationship becomes even more important if you think about where the world is going. I think we are increasingly moving to subscription services for everything.

Some fifteen years ago, subscriptions were limited to things like newspapers, magazines, the utilities in your home, and cable television. We now have food as a service. Blue Apron is a perfect case in point. If I want a box to show up at my house containing ingredients I can cook for dinner, that's what I get. Many retailers, like StitchFix, will send you outfits periodically for your selection and approval, then take back the ones you don't want. There is even a subscription razor blade service for shaving, and *transportation as a service* will be the norm before too long. (I'm talking about the next step beyond Uber, not a bus pass.)

The reality is that I think today's marketer needs to look at everything we consume, everything we buy, every bit of business we do, and think through it all using a lens that projects ten years into the future. By then, everything will be consumed as a service. Absolutely everything.

When that happens, of course, the key will be to hold on to your customers for as long as you possibly can.

UPSELLING AND CROSS-SELLING

When you think about customer acquisition, there's a term that is universally used in almost every industry: "Land and expand." It is certainly true in B2B.

There is a widely held belief that if we sell a product or service—even if we take a significant hit or discount on it—we will inevitably sell more products to that customer in the future. It's the profitability "red herring." (I'm talking about cross-selling, that is, selling additional products to an existing customer, or upselling, which is all about migrating them to a more expensive or add-on offering.)

But unless you have a clear engagement model and platform to involve those customers, that belief is the biggest fallacy in existence. The reality is that you cannot assert that "land and expand," a VERY popular notion in the software world, works—because it does not—unless you have a robust engagement model.

Creating long-term value is a science, not an art or a belief. It stems from business execution, continuous self-improvement, constant measurement, and rewarding your people based on value drivers.

For proof, you don't have to look beyond how many additional products you are selling your customers. Most organizations don't sell their existing customers more than one additional product or service. Every company I have worked for had the same long-tail graph for product adoption. The number of organizations using one or two products or services was very high, followed by a precipitous drop-off after that in terms of organizations that purchased three or more products.

Creating long-term value is a science, not an art or a belief. It stems from business execution, continuous self-improvement, constant measurement, and rewarding your people based on value drivers.

You can always find a handful of existing customers who will buy everything you offer. That's nirvana, of course. We want every one of the customers who do business with us to be like that. But that isn't going to happen consistently without an engagement platform.

If we are deeply engaged with a customer, if we understand their needs, if we understand their motivations, their timelines, their targets, their growth goals and objectives, if we have a model that is sensing—both digitally and physically—how our customers are evolving, we have a better chance of selling them more.

You can think of it as another rung on the lifetime value ladder that goes from acquisition to retention to growth to advocacy.

TIME, TIME, TIME IS ON OUR SIDE (YES, IT IS)

Let me give you an example of the kind of engagement I am talking about. It involves shifting our thinking from time-to-deployment to time-to-value.

We often measure how long it takes a customer to deploy or start using our product once they buy it from us. All companies have some sense of this timeline, but we don't typically know the time frame from when we first started engaging with a customer (aka when they were still a prospect) to when they derive value from our product. They will continue to do business with us over a long period only if they find value in what we are offering. Too often, we stop measuring once the customer makes an initial purchase. But coming back to my previous point on customer success, it doesn't do us any long-term good if people are not happy with what they bought. Are they using it? Some 60% of software is "shelfware" (yes, including cloud products). That is software that just sits unused, never deployed. (Shelfware is admittedly an old-school term as it literally meant "software that sat in a box, on a shelf, uninstalled." Not sure what to call cloud shelfware other than "wasted money"!) At Marketo, if customers are not using our product actively, there's a good chance that not only will they never buy anything else from us, they will cut the cord at the end of the contract term. That's why you want to measure time-to-value.

Notice the way I worded that: "Time" begins before you sell someone anything. Time begins when you start engaging. If you are bringing a potential customer a new idea, you are already providing value prior to a sale. That's why you need to focus on time to value. "How long did it take customers to receive value from us from the moment we first engaged?" (NOT the first MQL, Sales Qualified Lead, or sales call!) That's a great question to ask, because it forces the marketer to ponder things like, "What does the customer perceive as value?" and "How well are we delivering against their expectations?"

A lot of us who grew up in the software industry, and I will raise my hand here, were taught that a customer gets value the moment they turn on the product. But common sense tells you that this is not necessarily the case. To draw an analogy, if it is cold outside and you turn on the heat, you are not getting value the moment you flip the switch to "on." The value comes when the home is warm.

DIGGING DEEPER

Before we move on, we need to drill down into the sub elements of lifetime value.

If you think about how to calculate lifetime value in its simplest form, it is easy to understand. It's the profit a customer contributes times the length of time they are a customer (making that contribution), minus the acquisition costs.

Expressed as a formula, it looks like this:

Lifetime Value

=

The average profit contribution of the customer

×

the average number of years they stay with you

−

the initial cost of the customer acquisition.

If you look at it that way, then churn—how often customers leave you—becomes really important. You, of course, need to ruthlessly measure churn, because your customers ultimately vote with their wallets.

Now, you should be a little careful with lifetime value. Just because someone renews with you or buys from you again doesn't mean they're happy and are destined to be a brand advocate. We will talk about this a little bit later in the chapter, but the reality may be that they have no other option. They could be locked into a contract, for example. With that caveat, I think it's essential to understand churn rate and what drives customer churn (and retention, the other side of the same coin).

There is also a flip side that's important to understand. You need to drill into how long you are keeping your customers.

When you say you are going to hold on to a customer for life, you need to know what "life" means. Having a customer for longer than a decade is not unheard of. But in a world where the half-life of companies themselves is getting shorter, we need to acknowledge that the ability to hold on to a customer forever is shrinking as well.

I also think product discount rate should be calculated or thought about inside of lifetime value. When I use the phrase *discount rate*, I am not referring to it as the finance guys do (i.e., a way to adjust for present value). Rather, I am talking about the discount, or price reduction, you give to customers. The reality is that your discount rate should not continually increase in a highly valuable relationship. I think that any customer who recognizes value in a relationship is willing to spend more than a customer who views it as a commodity or low economic value-type relationship. That's a standard notion.

Another thing that you need to think about is how often you receive new revenue in terms of upsell and/or cross-sell from a customer.

A long-term value focus does not start with the CMO. A long-term value focus does not even start with the CEO. To me, it starts with the willingness of the board of directors to orient itself around a long-term strategy, and then the ability of the CEO and the CMO to act on that commitment.

BRAND ADVOCATES

When it comes to strategic metrics, brand advocates are intimately intertwined with long-term customer value.

We've established who advocates are at this point in the book, but in case you missed it, in short, they are your brand champions and are not shy about saying so.

To create an advocate, you must engage the customer across the life cycle to keep them successful. You need to live your brand promise in every interaction with them. Once you do both of those things, you have a better chance of getting—and keeping—advocates for your brand.

Consequently, creating, nurturing, and providing advocates a platform to socially promote their love for the brand is an essential and measurable strategy for success in the Engagement Economy.

CAN COMPANIES USE THE NET PROMOTER SCORE INSTEAD?

I often get asked if companies can use the Net Promoter Score (NPS) as a surrogate for brand advocates.

You could, but I don't recommend it.

As you know, NPS is a very simple measure. You ask people if they are positive, neutral, or negative about your brand. More specifically, you ask them how likely they are to recommend your brand to a friend or colleague.

That's fine. But it can be very easily manipulated.

First, the score can be wildly affected by who you ask.

Second, it can be wildly affected by how many people you include in your net promoter survey. Both those things can lead to a ridiculous amount of inconsistency in your score from year to year. You're never really comparing apples to apples.

I'm not pooh-poohing NPS, but I don't think it is the "gold standard" that it once was, because the world we live in just moves too fast! Let me give you an example to explain why.

Let's say that you run an NPS survey, and at the end of it, you find out you have a positive score and say, "Isn't that great?" Well, how do you then track whether or not those people are actively promoting your brand after the survey?

You don't. With brand advocates, you know they are tweeting something, or posting a comment, or writing a blog post.

Where did my belief come from? It was definitely a bit of an epiphany. I had probably just come out of the 10,000th sales and marketing meeting of my career, and I was once again frustrated. The marketing organization had just presented all kinds of data that showed it was hitting its goals. The sales department had explained that it was doing fine, and yet the company was struggling to hit its targets.

When someone pointed out that the company was struggling, marketing would say the sales force was terrible. The sales force would say that marketing wasn't generating enough high-quality leads. Finger-pointing central and, fundamentally, no alignment.

The epiphany happened while we were in this infinite loop of agreeing we needed more revenue, so we would run an additional campaign, hand the leads off to sales, and wait to see what happened. Then rinse, repeat, and rinse, repeat. There was never a conversation about how to gain leverage with the existing customer base to grow the organization.

What we were missing was a conversation about how we could use the *voice of our customers* to help promote and drive our brand in a responsible way. **The insight was that we had to build an army of brand advocates!**

I am certainly not the first person to think about the power of brand advocates. But what dawned on me was, while there were a number of people who were preaching this gospel as well as other concepts like earned media, etc., the reality was that most people didn't realize it involves an iceberg effect. For every single brand advocate you're aware of, there are ten more people below the waterline that you could turn into brand advocates. My bigger insight was that all these brand advocates were perhaps the most under-appreciated asset a marketer can access.

The big question, of course, is how do you prove that brand advocates are worth courting?

I'd start with a formal definition to share with your coworkers, which is more precise than the loose description I've provided so far. A brand advocate is a person who has a depth of conviction around your brand. From there, I would measure the activities of the advocates and compare them with typical customers who are not advocates, looking at things like profitability, how long they have been a customer, and the like. I think you'll come up with at least three observations.

One observation is that, if you have brand advocates, they are going to drive people who are evaluating your product or service to action—not just create awareness about the product, which is a traditional marketing activity. The second observation is that they will be with you for a long period. Third, they will be happier customers, and they, in turn, will recommend you to other people.

Invariably, you will find them to be far more profitable.

The reality is that a brand advocate is constantly providing ROI to the company. A single brand advocate is worth a thousand impressions. First, think of the time and cost it takes to create an impression. Then consider the shelf life of that impression. It is very short-lived.

In contrast, a brand advocate isn't costing you anything. They are marketing for you for free, and they are doing it on an ongoing basis. They are prolific creators of information, and the research shows just how valuable they can be.

- They create twice as many communications as the average customer about the brands they support or advocate for.

- They are generally savvier in terms of the quality of their communication. In fact, they are 70% more likely to be seen as a source of reliable information and three times as likely to share brand information with someone they don't know.

- They are more than twice as likely to share what they know to contribute to a pool of information.

My favorite statistic about this is: When asked if "people make purchases based on the information I provide," some 38% of web users said yes, and 57% of brand advocates said yes. That's a big difference.

ADVICE FOR THE NEW CMO

When you're a new CMO at an organization, I think it's reasonable to ask the CEO, "Why did you fire the old CMO? What was it that they were not doing?"

If the answer is, for example, "Well, they weren't generating enough leads" or "They weren't generating enough pipeline," I think the next reasonable question to ask is, "Are you going to provide me more budget to generate more opportunities?"

If the answer is no—which is generally the case, and, in fact, the answer more commonly is "You are going to have

(continued)

an even smaller budget"—then you are going to have to do things differently. Pursuing a model that calls for creating as many brand advocates as possible could be that different course.

If the CEO challenges you about your decision, you can ask one more question: "Do you want a virtual army of advocates that costs us a fraction of what we were spending on impressions and other vanity metrics? Or do you just want to keep going down the same (less than optimal) path we've been on?"

BENEFITS AND RISKS

The lingering power of a brand advocate success story is in how it outperforms any content or campaign that a marketer can develop. Customers who are operating and running things like blogs on your site will outperform anything you could post.

A second benefit is that a happy customer can generate a net new opportunity. A brand advocate can—more quickly than your salespeople—influence someone to buy.

Brand advocacy is a real thing. In a world where people don't want to be sold to, brand advocates are not *selling* your product; they are *encouraging* and *engaging with* their audience to get them to buy. Today, when people are frequently opting out of receiving messages from companies, brand advocates are profoundly less likely to be tuned out. Surveys show messages from brand advocates get through 90% as often.

WHILE BRAND ADVOCATES CAN BE WONDERFUL FOR YOUR BUSINESS, THERE ARE RISKS INVOLVED

For one thing, you can't control what your brand advocates say about you. If there is a flaw in your product or service, odds are people are going to talk about it. The second thing is that if you are not curating your brand advocate community (something we will discuss later), you can lose control of your message.

Finally, brand advocates can switch sides. An example in the soft drink wars would be switching from Coke to Pepsi. Switching sides can create significant risk, because the brand advocates who switch might be extremely credible and influential.

So, the risks are significant, but you can minimize them.

Identify who you want

Start by identifying who you want as a brand advocate. You need to do research, because—to pick an extreme example— you don't want a brand advocate who maintains a politically inflammatory page on Facebook. So, you need to thoroughly vet your brand advocates.

Talking doesn't equal influence

You also need to understand that just because someone talks a lot about your product doesn't mean they have a broad network or they are a strategic influencer. You need to understand this person's reach. That's part of the curation process. You want to spend most of your time with the people who reach the biggest audiences.

Employees can be brand advocates

Finally, as you are thinking about this, remember that employees can be excellent brand advocates. When you build a brand advocacy program, always start from the inside out by trying to turn your employees into brand advocates. Then you can move on to the outside world.

Once you've identified the people outside of your company who you want as advocates, and you have curated the list, you need to communicate with them clearly and frequently. You'll probably need to talk to them more than you do to your own employees at some level. Then close the loop by providing some sort of reward system for your advocates.

I am not talking about bribes or even going over the top. First, it isn't ethical. Second, either approach would probably alienate most of your advocates, who will tell you sincerely that they cannot be bought. They will tell you it's clear when someone's trying to buy, influence, or earn their opinion. There's a difference between liking someone's comment on Twitter and buying them a trip to Hong Kong.

With that in mind, you need a clear idea of how the reward program will work and what you will and will not do. Things like sending them a note or cool swag from your company strike me as fair. So does inviting them to attend your annual user conference at a discounted rate or for free because they've been such a positive brand advocate.

There's another nuance to be noted. There will be very different drivers (i.e., motivators) for your different types of brand advocates. What drives a Millennial is going to be very different from what drives a Gen Xer or a Baby Boomer.

ANOTHER SUBTLE PAYOFF

You always want to monitor your brand advocates. How active are they? What are they saying? Is their core sentiment improving, declining, or staying the same?

You may be able to use your brand advocates as a canary in the coal mine. If you're seeing your brand advocates' sentiment trend negative, there may be some underlying issue that you need to address.

So, it's about listening, it's about learning, and then, it's about engaging your own brand advocate program.

Let me take this discussion full circle. We began talking about brand advocates by pointing out how they can be a more effective tool than using an alternative like the Net Promoter Score. Let's end this discussion the same way. With brand advocates, you are building an army of virtual marketers, people who are willing to serve as your proxy on Twitter, Facebook, LinkedIn, and elsewhere. As long as you continue to stay aligned to your brand advocates, this virtual marketing organization will continue to promote your product or service.

I have yet to meet a marketer on this planet who would not be open to having hundreds, thousands, or tens of thousands of brand advocates posting on their behalf and sharing their passion for the company.

Creating such a force is something the marketer has day-to-day direct impact and control over through the process of engagement.

ONE MORE THING

There is one last point to make: Don't confuse your highest paying customers with your biggest brand advocates. A lot of times people who don't pay you a lot end up being your best brand advocates, because they're more passionate about your brand.

Microsoft did a study in a user community many years ago, and they found that the people who were most engaged in community were not necessarily the biggest customers. I think that happens a lot.

There are two key growth drivers going forward: Brand Advocacy and Customer Lifetime Value. Moving the organization forward begins with the CMO and CEO being aligned around those two metrics.

SEVEN

More Data = Better Engagement

What you'll learn in this chapter:

- Why B2B and B2C marketers need to understand their customers' "lifestyle."
- How "precision marketing" works.
- How to build a relationship of trust with your customers.
- Why you are still not personalizing your marketing enough.
- What you can learn from a tractor company. Hint: a lot.

More data equals better engagement. Okay, this should really say, "The better use of data and information equals better engagement," but that would be too long of a chapter title. As we explore this topic, let's start at a rawer level than "data." When we engage with people, it's more than just business. We are engaging with *people* . . . and every human being has needs, wants, and demands that extend beyond the workplace. Every human being has a lifestyle that is unique to them that plays into their values and ultimately their decision-making.

Consider a study by Bankrate.com on Millennials that sheds some light on their lifestyle choices versus those of Gen Xers or Baby Boomers. Millennials, for example, tend to spend significantly less money on homes and luxury goods (e.g., diamonds) yet spend notably more money on groceries and gas. (This is supposed to be the Toyota Prius generation!)

More specifically, on average, people between the ages of eighteen and thirty-six spend $2,300 more per year on groceries, gas, restaurants, and cell phone bills than those who are thirty-seven and older. Yet they spend $1,130 less on travel and television than their elders. Of course, you can attribute part of that to income. But the main premise of this chapter is this: Comprehending *lifestyle* in marketing and engagement is paramount to your ongoing success!

Over the last twenty years, and certainly within the last ten, we have observed that demographic or household data alone is not enough to truly know someone and understand their preferences. Even if you are armed with good probabilistic data, you (or someone in your organization) can make the wrong inferences—and often do.

Here's a simple example. Say you sell nutritional supplements and buy a list of the names of people who are members of 24 Hour Fitness (the health club chain). Marketing to those people would seem to make sense, but we don't know for certain that those people have an active lifestyle. We are inferring that they do consume supplements. However, we should consider that people on the list we purchased may not go to the gym that often. After all, a lot of people with gym memberships don't exercise that frequently. (Especially after their New Year's resolutions wear off.)

The reason we need to know more than how old someone is or whether they have a gym membership is that we want to invest our engagement and marketing dollars as wisely as possible. We've espoused, throughout this book, that building a digital persona or profile of an individual is paramount to your success. Furthermore, I asserted that keeping that persona evergreen and continually refined is of equal import. To that end, let's explore some means by which you can build out a more comprehensive digital persona of a buyer (or account).

You can take two different data-driven approaches to better engage your audience: inferential and deterministic.

Inferential marketing (or targeting) is exactly what it sounds like. We find out a handful of things about you, and we make assumptions from there based on a more generic set of data. For example, we learn you are between twenty-five and thirty-five, you're male, and you have a gym membership. From there, we assume you have an active lifestyle and are likely to buy nutritional supplements. As we just saw, those assumptions may or may not be true. In other marketing scenarios, inferential data is used to infer that I am the same person across an iPhone and an iPad visiting your website, even though you lack empirical proof.

In deterministic marketing (or targeting), marketers go to great lengths to build a digital persona or profile that contains definitive proof of a consumer's identity. Deterministic marketing solutions rely only on known facts about people, typically revealed via a login, IP address, or cross-matched device profile. Adding quantifiable and qualitative information about your customers and prospects, including their lifestyle focus, will help you drive more accuracy into your engagement and marketing.

And by the way, how we leverage both inferential and deterministic approaches to engagement is the topic of this chapter!

I think most marketers are still operating in the world of inferential marketing. This isn't a bad thing, and it's generally easier than the deterministic approach. But it limits the precision with which we can engage. It necessitates appealing to a broader swath of buyers (vs. individuals) in general.

If I haven't given it away yet, I am a big fan of a deterministic approach.

Now, "lifestyle" data can seem somewhat qualitative vs. quantitative, ergo at odds with a deterministic approach to targeted engagement, but I think they are congruent. Understanding someone's lifestyle requires more than two or three demographic data points to drive real precision targeting. Let's take me. I'm forty-five years old. I like to exercise quite a bit—five to six days per week—but I wouldn't say I orient my lifestyle *around* fitness (e.g., I'm not someone who works out two hours or more per day). I enjoy travel. I have a modest level of addiction to health drinks and protein shakes. When you look at this data, you gain a fuller picture of me and can create a more tailored pitch. I am telling you all this about me because, as you will see later in the chapter, someone used all this data to make a very effective B2B pitch to me.

The reason we should include lifestyle data in digital persona creation is simply to avoid making incorrect assumptions. Let's go back to Millennials for a moment. All marketers make assumptions when they describe an individual as a Millennial, and often those assumptions are wrong. I asked a few marketers to describe attributes of Millennials to me based on data they've gathered.

Here's what they shared:

- They are more liberal and left-leaning politically than the general population,

- They do not trust "the system," and

- They are probably more extroverted than introverted.

Those are just some points that jumped off the page for me. Some of those statements may be true for some Millennials, but then again, not all Millennials are the same. For example, while Millennials are generally more active on social media than other groups, 25% of them *don't* have any social media accounts.

There are two points to make here: One, as marketers we tend to be very assumptive or presumptive. And two, in the Engagement Economy, we must move toward being deterministic and precise. *In other words, we really have to understand not just someone's values but the actual lifestyle of the person we want to engage.*

Stephanie Meyer, CMO of Connecture, a healthcare IT and solutions company, captured this thought well when we talked to her.

"I don't believe in engagement for the sake of engagement," she said. "You need to customize your engagement. For example, my twenty-one-year-old son, who lives with me, gets the same flyers from health insurance providers as I do. Clearly, he and I belong to two different segments, yet we're being marketed to with the same content."

For me, the nirvana of marketing information, beyond household and demographic data, would be a complete understanding of what a typical week looks like for the person I am targeting. That's a very different question to ask from "Do you have a gym membership?" Knowing how someone spends an extended block of their time can produce a great deal of qualitative and quantitative information.

We can even ask that question about corporations, because businesses also have a lifestyle. For example, the lifestyle at Facebook is likely quite different from the lifestyle at IBM. So, we are not just talking about the individual—in the world of B2B, we are also talking about the firm where those individuals work. Wouldn't it be incredibly helpful to know what a workweek looks like for someone at AT&T? For someone at General Motors? At Lyft?

> We as marketers love labels. We love them because they make our lives easier. But easy is not the answer.

That said, most marketers don't do this simply because they are unsure of the return on the investment. I'm not calling anyone lazy, because they aren't. It's just that I think we operate too much at the inferential level based on overarching labels like *liberal, conservative, Millennial, Baby Boomer,* or whatever. These labels are very powerful and can cause us to shift into assumptive mode. Furthermore, our broad labels cut completely against the grain of what we're saying in this book, which is that you truly need to know your customers and engage with them on a deep and meaningful level.

While we may love labels because they make our lives easier, easy is not the answer.

IS GETTING DETAILED CREEPY? NO

In the abstract, gathering household, demographic, values, and lifestyle data on your customers can strike some as intrusive. But if done right, collecting this data to build knowledge, then using it wisely, doesn't have to be invasive. Ultimately, there is no difference between how you get to know someone in the digital world and in the physical world.

To understand why building a more "intimate" digital persona of a customer is not intrusive, ask yourself if you have a relationship of trust with specific brands. The answer is that you probably do—whether it's with your credit card company, or a company like Amazon. Like it or not, these companies must know an awful lot about you to deliver a meaningful level of engagement.

Think about the way those companies engage with you. Do you (generally) find it annoying or intrusive? Probably not. Granted, they are selective in terms of how they engage with customers, which begets a relationship of trust over time.

There is little difference between how you build a digital relationship of trust and a physical one. If you meet someone for the first time and have a great conversation, there is still a long list of awkward questions that you *could* ask them, things that would either be too prying or too personal. But you *don't*. We just innately sense that. There are certain places you know not to go to.

It's no different when you build that relationship digitally. There are certain places you know are off limits. Follow your human instincts—the ones you employ in the physical world—in the digital realm.

Here's the challenge that we as marketers face. We are armed with incredibly powerful digital platforms that enable us to gather personal data on individuals. I am, in fact, recommending that we gather even more data on people. That said, I am also advocating that we respect the privacy of the individual and the data we gather.

The modern digital marketer needs to establish a trust model that is adhered to throughout the organization. They could even publish this model for the sake of transparency. How do you build a trust model? You can start with a model used outside of marketing for data itself: the 4 Vs of big data—volume, variety, velocity, and value.

Let's start with volume, and let me ask you a question. If you purchased something from me one time, does this give me the right to send you ten marketing emails per week? How about if you purchased ten items? Can I send you an email once or twice per day? The answer in both cases is obviously no. I haven't earned that right. Yet hundreds of thousands of organizations violate that notion all the time. By breaking the "volume" rule, they never establish trust.

On velocity, which is the frequency of engagement (across multiple digital channels), the question is *when* does engagement occur. As a customer, if you indicated you'd be okay receiving five emails per month from my company, is it alright if I send them all on the second Friday of the month? How likely is someone to open five emails from the same company on the same day? Yet companies send them!

Then there's variety of engagement. Just because you purchased something from me, does that give me the right to follow you on Facebook, LinkedIn, Twitter, Google, and the like? No. In fact, that *is* super creepy. It's like being digitally stalked. It's unnerving, and it certainly doesn't build trust. That said, you can certainly *ask* buyers or customers for their permission . . . that's a different ball game.

Finally, there's value. Is what you are communicating valuable to your audience? Is there something in it for them? Just because I provide a service, like selling you a car, doesn't give me the right to ask you to rate me a perfect 10 should the parent company follow up to see how I did. That's a violation of trust. I'm effectively asking you to lie for me—which is not engaging.

In the research Marketo commissioned in the US and UK, some 82% of marketers in B2B and B2C companies believed that they had a deep understanding of how their customers want to be engaged. Yet in stark contrast, only 33% of their B2B customers thought that was the case.

WHEN YOU COMPILE THE DATA

When you build a digital persona or profile, you should start by defining what kind of information you are looking for. First, there's the demographic/household information that you should have on hand. Usage data from websites, mobile, etc. is all fair game and should be included.

But before you go compiling everything, there may be an easier way to go about determining what information you want to find. Ask three questions:

- Who are our brand advocates today?

- Why do they advocate for our company?

- What data have we captured regarding our brand advocates?

Do you have enough information to understand what is valuable to a brand advocate? Exploring this question will lead you down the path of understanding how you create more brand advocates. You can create a template and build off that.

AN EXAMPLE OF A COMPANY THAT HAS DONE THIS WELL

To see a company that has mastered an understanding of its customers, let's look at a 180-year-old tractor company: John Deere. It is both a B2B and B2C company. It sells to individual farmers as well as to huge agricultural firms. My grandfather owned a John Deere tractor on his tobacco farm in West Virginia, and even the name *John Deere* makes me smile, because I can picture him in work overalls and a John Deere hat. To me, there's something warm and humanistic about the brand—it somehow feeds the soul.

You can see that John Deere understands its customers' lifestyle from the way it positions itself in branding, advertising, support, and service.

Yet, I don't believe that the company is marketing or selling tractors and farm equipment—what it is really selling is a promise. The promise is that if you buy from John Deere, you will maximize the yield of your agricultural or farming efforts, and one of the ways you will get there is through things like zero downtime.

In a moment, I will elaborate on how John Deere delivers on that promise. But first it is worth noting that a John Deere tractor can cost anywhere from tens of thousands to hundreds of thousands of dollars! If you're an individual farmer, that's no small buy. The large commercial farms will spend tens of millions of dollars, and sometimes hundreds of millions of dollars, on fleets of these things. Farming is big business, so how does John Deere keep it personal?

To serve these customers better, Deere has transformed its marketing efforts. It started with technology, putting sensors on all its tractors. Today, an individual tractor will have literally hundreds (and possibly thousands) of sensors installed on it, monitoring how well the machine is per-forming—everything from tire pressure to temperature. Thus, through the magic of IoT (the Internet of Things), the company can detect from thousands of miles away when the alternator, for example, is going to fail. It knows days and sometimes weeks before that failure is going to happen, because aberrant data is fed over a cellular network back to John Deere's headquarters.

When Deere employees see this information, they're able to reach out to the farmer, engage, and potentially say, "We'd like to fix your tractor." I can imagine the hypothetical conversation with the farmer, who's insisting that the tractor isn't broken. Yet John Deere is able to say, "But it will be tomorrow!"

What this means is the first level of engagement from the perspective of the company is recognizing *when* there is going to be a problem. The second level of engagement is suggesting times for the repair when the machinery would have been otherwise idle. So, John Deere is delivering on its promise of zero downtime.

John Deere is a 180-year-old tractor company that is no longer a tractor company. It's an engagement company. It's a software company. It's a company that delivers on the promise of "We will maximize your yield" by being proactive (as we saw above) and by delivering real-time data like weather information and yield information (when to plant, soil quality, and moisture content).

Marketers need to drive fundamental, unique, and valuable engagement, and that's exactly what companies like John Deere are doing. You may say, "Steve, this isn't marketing."

I believe it is. *It's most certainly engagement.* There are no ads you can place online to supersede the engagement I just described!

STORING AND COLLATING

When you begin to build out more robust profiles of your customers and accounts, it's natural to turn to your CRM system, given you may view it as your customer data system of record.

While that's standard practice for many organizations, there's a huge difference between a contact database and CRM. A contact database is exactly what it sounds like. It's a database where you store as much information as you can collect about your contacts, such as their name, how they like to be contacted, information preferences, and more. It can even include things like existing communications to and from your customer, as well as their responses. Of course, you'll also find demographic and household data (i.e., age, birth date, gender, profession, etc.).

There are a few other things I think you should also add. Social graph data (i.e., who's connected to whom), product preferences, lifestyle info, and, of course, whether they pay their bills on time. We usually just market to everybody, and we don't think that we should focus marketing efforts on organizations with the best net terms or the least number of Day Sales Outstanding (DSOs). We should.

Most people don't think of storing customer information the way we just discussed. They immediately equate CRM with a contact database. You may disagree on the difference, but CRM, as we've discussed, is customer relationship management software, not contact management software. Does CRM include a contact database? Yes. But the CRM product you're using may not have the level of maturity, in terms of contact attributes, support for metadata, and customizability that you need.

All this said, here are the rules for storing data to help you better engage.

- First, understand what data will aid in building a deeper or more lasting relationship with your customer.

- Second, make sure that your company has a clear understanding of the myriad data privacy laws relative to that data. (*Especially* global data privacy laws.)

Marketers tend to put the cart in front of the horse on this one, especially when it comes to GDPR (General Data Protection Regulation, a set of data privacy laws set by the EU that were implemented in May of 2018). We want to collect as much data as we can on the customer, but we don't often contemplate securing it. Furthermore, we don't think enough about what would happen to our company from a liability standpoint if that data were exposed.

SQUISHY?

Sometimes, after listening to all this, people tell me they understand—in theory—why you would want to gather "lifestyle" data on your customers and potential customers. But they feel it is "too squishy" and that their marketing dollars could be best spent elsewhere. When they say that, they're forgetting the fact that every buyer in a B2B or B2C scenario is a real human being. Real human beings experience life events that affect their behavior.

All the digital information and marketing technology at our command has given us unprecedented insight into the end-to-end lifestyle of a human being. When leveraged responsibly, this knowledge allows us to form a deeper relationship with our customers, which fosters loyalty to our brands.

Let me give you an example that blew me away recently.

I spoke at a conference put on by one of our partners in Las Vegas, and I stayed at the MGM Grand Hotel. When I got to my room, there was a chocolate sculpture of the Marketo logo—I love chocolate—and a note that said three things:

> *Mr. Lucas, we know you are speaking at the confer-ence tomorrow, and we at the MGM are thrilled to host you.*

(Remember, it wasn't Marketo's conference. I was just a keynote speaker.)

> *We enjoyed the article about your passion for Cross-Fit that appeared in* The Silicon Valley Business Journal. *In your room refrigerator, you'll find two pro-tein shakes with our compliments. And we want you to know that our gym opens at 5:00 am.*

> *We certainly would love to speak with you about the opportunity to host your Marketing Nation event two years from now.*

(They didn't say next year, because somehow they already knew we were going to be hosting that event in San Francisco in 2018.)

Now, THAT'S the kind of engagement I'm talking about!

I had never met these people in my life. Never. Yet, they knew I was speaking at the event and that I enjoy exercise. So, they made the effort to tell me about the gym, which eliminated the need for me to pick up the phone to ask the front desk what time it opened. Instead of the standard Pringles® and jelly beans, they gave me a couple of protein shakes, something I happen to love that also fits my lifestyle.

Then, yes, there was a B2B ask, which was, "We'd love you to consider the MGM in two years." Not too shabby, MGM!

Independent research we commissioned shows that "personalization is one of the most important methods brands can use to effectively engage customers."

Now undoubtedly, the hotel had to do some media and social homework to get this level of information about me. But obviously, it had some initial intel on hand, and the rest was not all that hard to find.

Did I find this intrusive? Not at all! I found the approach to be a welcome one, and I am not alone in being receptive to this kind of TLC. As one B2B buyer told our researchers, "I will be happier when brands interact with me on a more personalized level. When they do, I am more likely to have a great relationship with them."

> Independent research we commissioned shows that "personalization is one of the most important methods brands can use to effectively engage customers."

One last point about leveraging lifestyle information in your engagement efforts: It's not solely about the data and the quality of the data. It's also about building a behavioral model of your buyer using algorithms and mathematics. That is where marketing is unequivocally going. We are on the cusp of being able to accurately predict, with precision, whether a person is in a buying mood or not, solely based on digital behavior!

I put a tremendous amount of weight on data and information, but what I put more weight on is what you do with the data, something we will talk about in the next chapter.

HOW DO YOU PROVE THIS APPROACH IS HELPFUL?

If marketers are good at one thing, they're good at A/B testing. For a marketer reading this book who is not using lifestyle data today and confident that this data will add value, then I have some great news. You can start testing it! Start compiling and using lifestyle data as part of your marketing efforts. Then compare the results in terms of retention rates, revenue, conversions, ROMI, lead generation, and more to the marketing efforts that leverage standard demographic and firmographic data. Most customers I talk to about this start by using lifestyle data for their most important clients and marquee accounts—which is a great idea.

USING INFORMATION TO CREATE ADVOCATES

Marketing in the Engagement Economy should be a five-step process. In my mind, the first four areas are as fundamental as motherhood and apple pie:

1. You're educating customers and prospective customers.

2. To some degree, you're entertaining them.

3. You're inspiring them to take action.

4. Ultimately, you're converting them to buy.

But you shouldn't stop there. You want to add a fifth step—an *invitation*. That's the new rule in the world of social media and social marketing. You want your customers to contribute to creating content and sharing their experiences with your brand. Isn't that what we ultimately want? Don't we ultimately want an army of advocates not on our payroll creating content for us? You won't get that unless you *invite* them to contribute.

There are two types of invitations. One is, "If you do this, I will give you 50% off" or some other inducement. That, to me, is disingenuous. You are buying their advocacy. Then, there's the invitation where you start small. You ask people to share their experience with your company. Then you can ask if they would share their experience with another potential customer, and you go from there.

Isn't there a problem in offering the invitation? No, because before you ask them to engage, you must earn the right to engage, which implies you've provided them with the right experience and correct level of interaction in the past.

Now, again, you should truly understand how a potential advocate wants to promote you (i.e., the channel of choice through which they want to advocate). Some will be comfortable as one-to-one references. In a B2B situation, some customers are comfortable with taking a reference call. Someone else might be very comfortable going on Facebook and posting, "I love this brand." My personal favorite is inviting advocates to author a small blog post about interacting with your company. Others might be comfortable sharing a post on LinkedIn or linking to an article. I have found most advocates enjoy attending your user conference and sharing their perspectives in a one-to-many forum. The bottom line is you should understand the channels of advocacy choice and use engagement technology at scale to facilitate their sharing.

MOVING BEYOND CUSTOMERS FOR LIFE

For the longest time, the Holy Grail when it came to customer service was creating "customers for life." If you did a great job satisfying your customers, the thinking went, those

(continued)

customers would stick with you forever. Nothing was greater than that.

Well, that was then; this is now.

Yes, of course, you want to create customers for life, but you don't want to stop there. The whole idea is to get to the point where your customers (for life) become your brand advocates and help you attract even more customers. One of the ways you can get there is by asking yourself, *"How do I create an experience that results in my customers lining up to create content for me"—whether that content is reviews of our products, or a blog post based on their experience, or something else?*

Here's the bottom line. It starts with an invitation. If you don't invite them, then it's difficult to get people to contribute.

Let's say I were to invite a Marketo customer to contribute content—a blog post—to our Marketing Nation community website. By doing so, I am telling them three things:

1. I value them as a customer.

2. I respect their opinion.

3. I trust them to produce content that is valuable to the rest of the community.

Clearly, in return, what they're getting for that is great exposure to the community where they will be perceived as a thought leader. But it all starts with an invitation to someone whose lifestyle you really understand!

EIGHT

The Engagement Life Cycle

What you'll learn in this chapter:

- Why the need for engagement is driving marketing's evolution.
- What the "infinite engagement life cycle" looks like.
- How to engage at every part of the customer's journey.
- Why process is everything.
- Why a honeybee may be your best role model.

At this point, one question invariably arises: Why is engagement better than marketing?

The answer is: It isn't. *One isn't better than the other.* But the reality is that some significant aspects of marketing haven't evolved very much over the past one hundred years, and they must today, given the speed of business. (Case in point: You can still get coupons in the mail, and many people still do.) Engagement is a key part of marketing's evolution, which makes sense, since we are in the Engagement Economy!

Engagement and experience are two sides of the same coin that comprise the new marketing ethos. Given this book focuses on engagement primarily, it's natural that you will want to know what changes you need to make to thrive in this new environment.

> Engagement and experience are two sides of the same coin that comprise the new marketing ethos.

There are several things to consider. First, let's talk funnels. The funnel image I shared back in chapter 1 represents how we were educated to think about the marketing and sales process. I'll reprise it here.

If you see a funnel or journey model that looks like one of these models when in your next marketing or sales planning meeting, a change is definitely in order!

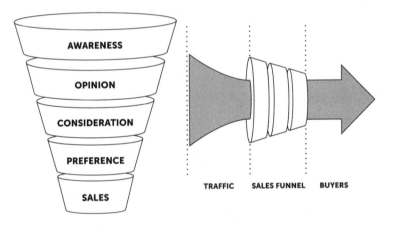

Figure 8.1 Typical funnel for marketing and sales.

According to what we were taught, there's a beginning and end in these funnels (or journey models). Things flow from top to bottom—or side to side, depending on how the funnel is drawn—in an orderly fashion. Yet we inherently know as marketers this is not the case in the Engagement Economy.

A proper and updated engagement process model looks like this:

Figure 8.2 Here's the infinite engagement life cycle, the right way to think about engaging customers forever.

Why this image? Two reasons. First, it charts what the actual buying process looks like today. The fact that we draw it with no beginning or end is also by design. It indicates exactly how long you should be thinking about retaining your customer: forever.

The graphic also acts as a guide for how you can begin to architect your marketing organization (and other departments) around engagement.

JOB #1

Before you do anything else, you'll want to informally survey the landscape in your organization. How does your company engage with customers, prospects, employees, and partners today? If you mapped it, would it look like our infinity symbol above?

To find out, I suggest you start by interviewing your peers as well as the heads of product, sales, customer success, services, and support. Ask them how "experience" is curated for the customer within their department as well as in the organization.

Next, ask how they think your organization engages with each of the following individually: customers, prospects, employees, and partners. Finally, ask them for ideas on ways you could better engage with all those people.

From those discussions, you should now have a solid framework to start filling in the life cycle model for your own company. Here it is again, with a few departments dropped in at different points in the process, along with a few ideas of how different groups might engage with your customers.

Figure 8.3 The engagement life cycle with marketing, sales, customer success, and account management applied. (This could easily be altered to include your product and customer support organizations.)

Think for a moment about how marketing plays a role in every part of the life cycle. (Hint: If it doesn't, there is a problem.) If you are the CMO or a marketing practitioner, do you play a role in engagement throughout your organization? If not, why not?

Glenn Thomas, CMO of GE Healthcare, explains why charting this engagement life cycle is so important. "It's paradoxical how digitization has simplified so much but also resulted in massive complexity of choice and demands for our finite level of attention. The approach Steve Lucas sets out can help marketers be more impactful by moving from simply being the loudest, to being the most *relevant* and *engaging* voice."

The payoff from employing this kind of life cycle charting can be huge. Listen to Brian Carrier, Vice President, Global Revenue Marketing and Marketing/Data Technology at Xerox. "We have transformed how we engage with our customers throughout the entire life cycle. Based on our evolving ability to track their interactions and transactions with us, coupled with an 'always on' understanding of their customer profiles, we can optimize their engagement across channels and understand their needs. We then deliver content and sales offers to help them understand Xerox's differentiated value. As a result, Xerox is able to acquire new logo business, offer additional services, and identify upsell and cross-sell opportunities. With this highly targeted approach, we've driven a 146% increase in engagement with our customers and exceeded industry benchmarks."

COMMON REACTIONS

When I share this model with marketers, I typically get three responses:

1. We don't have an engagement life cycle or strategy, but we try to engage (i.e., their approach is haphazard).

2. We do engage, but each department or group in our company controls their portion of engagement, so our overall engagement is disjointed. (Which, of course, leads to a disjointed customer experience).

3. No one at my company owns or stewards engagement for the company end to end.

If you would respond similarly, the good news is you're not alone! That said, if you want to thrive, *none* of those responses is acceptable in the Engagement Economy. We must actively engage at every point in the customer journey—pre-sale, post-sale, and at every point in between.

Let me share a "Zen" example of this.

I was sitting outside at a lovely resort in Carmel, California, during a break at a management offsite meeting. It was a sunny day, and the flowers were in bloom. While I am not an expert on flora, I did notice there were at least a dozen different kinds in various colors—purple, yellow, white, red, even orange. (Since I'm not an expert at flora, "orange" seems like a good classification for a flower to me.)

Because this is the way my mind works, I suddenly compared all those flowers to the different digital properties and ways we, as marketers, offer points of engagement for our customer.

Extending the analogy further, their location became important. Some were close to the hotel lobby (i.e., headquarters) and others were further out. Then, there was their physical size and appearance: Some were brighter and bigger than others, just like some touchpoints will be of more importance to certain customers than others. Then I noticed a small honeybee sampling the nectar in one of the flowers. Bees, by nature, seldom fly in linear patterns. This bee seemed to spend a lot of time on one type of flower. (After the fact, I asked and was told it was a desert mallow. I can neither confirm nor deny the accuracy of that, but it sure sounds right.)

I sat there and tried to predict, based on the bee's obsession with that flower, if it would continue visiting that type of flower or if it would visit all the varieties available. I spent about five minutes studying its movements. (Then, I got bored.)

But I learned three things:

- The flight of the bee was erratic most of the time and only occasionally predictable.

- It did seem to prefer the desert mallow but didn't hesitate to sample other flowers.

- Mapping the flight of the bee wasn't impossible, but if you did, it would look like a squiggle, because the path he took was non-linear.

Undoubtedly, you've jumped to the punch line on why I am spending so much time describing a bee. It's a perfect representation of our customers' journey in the Engagement Economy. It's non-linear and often seems unpredictable and erratic.

That said, our customers, like that bee, still follow patterns and show preferences. They're just smaller patterns that are harder to spot. They buzz from one site to another, one app to another, one device to another, sampling the information that strikes their fancy. Buyers spend more time engaged on some sites than others. Just like with the bee, those patterns and preferences are difficult to map as well as understand, and it takes a tremendous amount of patience to really learn what they like. But in the Engagement Economy, we must make the effort!

Dewayne Hankins, Chief Marketing Officer for the Portland Trail Blazers, gets this in spades! "Our fans have various relationships with us; some are old fans, some are new fans, and all these different aspects to our fan base require a different way to engage with them. Understanding where a fan is in his relationship with the basketball team helps drive our decision-making and how we engage with them."

The takeaway here is that we should demonstrate the patience to observe the behavior of our customers and prospects and understand their preferences, values, and patterns. We also must be willing to let the bee (*ahem*, the buyer) guide itself on a journey, land on the sites it prefers, use the apps and devices it loves, all while being led toward the nectar (i.e., the sale)!

Okay, enough with the bee analogy. No doubt you are thinking, "If the buyer journey is non-linear, even erratic, why try and apply a process?" Well, the process is more about the curation of the experience and the architecting of engagement. Having a well-defined process enables us to think about how all the different parts/functions/groups in our company must engage during the buyer's journey.

Beyond the departments that participate in engagement, we should also consider the types of activities that occur at each phase of engagement.

In this next figure, we can begin to map out a buyer journey in more granular detail.

The following graphic isn't meant to be prescriptive in terms of each activity. It's more to serve as a construct for you to fill in as you think about your organization. Where do you and your department play a role? In what activities? What are the outcomes you want to see at each phase of the journey?

Figure 8.4 Examples of engagement activities in the engagement life cycle.

As you map a buyer's journey, you'll see that the appearance of "brand advocates" happens late in the cycle. That's because brand advocates require the most amount of time to develop.

What I love more than anything about this model is the fact that it can also serve as a way for you to benchmark the level of engagement maturity within your organization. Once you've mapped out activities and desired outcomes for each phase, you can rate your level of readiness using a red/yellow/green scale.

You may be thinking, *I am going to end up with a thirty-page document if I go through every phase of figure 8.4, outlining three to five outcomes per phase and then rating my organization on each!* Yeah. That's right. That is the level of detail you should be willing to create in order to win!

An organization that engages effectively with its customers has a mature, well-thought-out engagement strategy. I've given you the map to an effective engagement plan.

But I would also suggest that you do more and conduct engagement workshops. Gather people from different parts of your organization—marketing, sales, customer success, product, support, and the like—to map out your engagement plan end to end. This should not be a one-time exercise. This is something you need to revisit throughout the year, striving to improve every time. Again, this kind of effort is what it takes to win in the Engagement Economy. I can assure you that if you don't do this, your competitors will.

OUT OF THIS WORLD

Beyond the process and model I've shared, let's think in the abstract for a moment. Let's use our solar system as another metaphor for a buyer's journey to try to more fully understand how engagement works today.

Let's say the sun, which is at the center of the solar system, represents your company. Our goal as marketers is to reach out into the vastness of space and "attract" objects (i.e., buyers) to us. (Remember, we're the sun. Things orbit the sun.) The reality of this scenario is that most marketers don't think to reach beyond the third rock from the sun (i.e., Earth). We assume the buyer journey starts much closer to home than it really does. Why? Because the solar system is a really big place, and it's hard to get your head wrapped around the vast distances of outer space.

Here's a case in point: NASA sent a spacecraft called the *New Horizons* to visit the dwarf planet Pluto (it was just a "planet" when I was growing up). *New Horizons* traveled at 36,373 mph—the fastest spacecraft to ever be launched from Earth. Even traveling at that incredible speed, it took *New Horizons* nine years, five months, and twenty-five days to reach Pluto, which is roughly three billion miles away.

My point is this. Years ago, the buyer journey in our solar system would have started *much* closer to home, because technology limited our ability to travel to the farther reaches of the solar system. That said, technology has advanced so radically that what we thought was impossible twenty years ago is now not just possible, but in many cases, already achieved.

Interestingly, these days, the Internet, in terms of its sheer size and the amount of activity going on within it, is somewhat similar in complexity to our solar system. Facebook alone hosts billions upon billions of interactions and events every day. The expanse is massive, frankly too big to comprehend! Since we're human, we as marketers tend to focus on what's going on closest to home—our website, email, and social presence—because it's easier to think in a context our brains can easily understand. But in the Engagement Economy, it's the small touches that may happen, billions of miles away, that can alter purchase decisions months, even years, from now!

With our digital universe constantly expanding, we have to concern ourselves with what's occurring at the outer reaches of our digital frontier. The buyer visits so many places before they even get close to the warmth of our sun that we need to be ready to engage anywhere in the digital universe!

Speaking of massive amounts of information and sheer size,

one last thing I'd like to add: No marketer will be successful in the Engagement Economy without the aid of more advanced technology. Just as technology itself has expanded our universe, we must upgrade our use of it to extend our reach into that universe and understand its ever-changing shape. You're going to need some really smart software. Software so smart that it can think for itself.

That's where we turn next.

NINE

The Marketer and the Machine

 In this chapter, you'll learn about the following concepts:

- What the *Iron Man* movies can teach us about marketing technology.

- Why engagement requires not only the right tools but also the ability to track their effectiveness.

- How to select the right tools.

- Why Artificial Intelligence will disrupt everything (in a good way).

- Why you must master the technology (or accept the fact you—and your company—will fail).

Ever watch one of the *Iron Man* movies with Robert Downey Jr.? If so, do you recall the scenes where the character he plays, Tony Stark, dons the Iron Man suit and is immediately super-powered? The person and the machine are better together. It will be just the same in the future as marketers and the "machines" they use grow closer. In other words, the marketer and the machine are more powerful together.

The future of marketing, especially in a B2B context, is Artificial Intelligence (AI). Before you run out and get an AI-based marketing solution, it's important to understand that the number one challenge facing marketers today is the complexity of all the technology they use in their "stack." As one customer told us as part of the research I am about to talk about, "The top challenge facing marketers today is related to technology and the tools available to successfully manage customer engagement."

Again, back to our Marketo research, which found that satisfaction with current engagement tools was low. It ranged from 49% to 57% depending on what product we were talking about.

The dissatisfaction was across the board. Marketers said they found a lack of tools for what they needed, and the tools that did exist were too complex and too hard to employ and manage. Not surprisingly, they also said they were experiencing problems demonstrating a return on their marketing technology investment. Specifically, they commented that they were experiencing challenges with the following:

- Turning data into action,

- Demonstrating value, and

- Defining metrics.

Marketers realize that successful customer engagement requires them to acquire the right tools and track the effectiveness of their efforts. That's the good news. The bad news is that they are having problems doing both.

Marketing automation, which is important today, is going to become vital going forward. The tools and options available to us are going to increase, and while it may seem incomprehensible given today's landscape, so is their complexity. In fact, our good friend Scott Brinker of chiefmartech.com has assembled a slide that's well known in the industry. It shows over 5,000 logos of marketing technology companies.

The field of marketing technology has bloomed like the peak of cherry blossom season in Japan. Over the past five years, thousands of different, colorful varieties of software-as-a-service (SaaS) offerings have popped up across every category and sub-category of marketing and advertising. We call them martech and adtech for shorthand.

It's breathtaking to witness so much innovation.

In a very real sense, this massive array of marketing software helps us quantify just how dramatically marketing has changed—and is still changing. Almost all these solutions are offering net new capabilities that weren't a part of marketing's arsenal a decade ago.

Marketing is in a period of extraordinary transformation, and the expansive martech and adtech landscape is demonstrable evidence of the stunning scale of this revolution.

But there's some beast with this beauty too.

Sifting through this landscape can be daunting. How do you pick the right solutions? How do you get them to work together with the rest of your marketing technology systems (i.e., your marketing stack)? This has been a challenge for many marketers.

Luckily, the situation is improving. Major marketing software providers, such as Marketo, have increasingly become "platforms" that serve as a common foundation for these more specialized martech and adtech products.

What's a platform? Think of the iOS for your iPhone (or Android phone if you prefer). Those are mobile device platforms. You can easily add all kinds of apps to tailor your phone to work exactly as you want it to. Buy an app, it installs quickly and reliably, and it just works.

Marketing software platforms aren't quite that simple—at least not yet—but the general idea is the same. Your core marketing platform serves as the backbone of your marketing stack and your system of record for campaigns and customer data. You can plug in certified martech and adtech applications, and they integrate smoothly into your platform right from the outset.

Granted, there's still a lot of possible add-on applications to choose from. But once you select your core marketing platform, you can start to narrow the field. You can look for solutions that promote a certified integration with your platform. You can hear from other marketers on the same platform about the solutions they've found work best. There's a sweet spot where you have choices—but not too many choices.

Nonetheless, you may wonder if the overall martech landscape will continue to be this large. It's a good question.

On one hand, forces of market consolidation are steadily eliminating products that aren't the best or second-best at what they do. On the other hand, new innovations continue to spring up in marketing, inspiring entrepreneurs to introduce new products into the space.

But whether the overall landscape shrinks or grows, adopting a platform-based strategy gives you the opportunity to adapt to whatever changes the future brings.

That means we have a lot of choices, but it also means it's left to us to connect all those disparate technologies into something resembling an integrated "stack." If you ever wanted to know why marketing or campaign attribution is so difficult to track, it's in large part due to the complexity of marketing tools and technology.

That's the downside.

The upside? All these new tools, options, and approaches potentially can make us more effective than we have ever been and give us the ability to take care of customers better than we ever have. Hence, the Iron Man suit analogy.

What I've been alluding to throughout the book is that your marketing "stack" should evolve into an Engagement Platform. And yes, AI will play a big role in enhancing engagement.

With that, by way of context, we are going to discuss several things in this chapter. We will talk about where the market is today in terms of marketing technology, discuss where marketing technology is going in the immediate future, and outline where the industry is going medium to long term. We will also discuss how AI will literally transform the way your company does business.

Let's start with the world today.

WHERE WE ARE

Marketers in both the US and UK report that their digital marketing spend has grown in the past couple of years. You can see that pronounced increase in social media, email, web content, and more online advertising efforts.

Marketers see the increased digital spending to personalize their messages and "meet customers where they are." Technologies can listen to prospect and customer activities through digital channels, amass data, and turn it into information and insights. Then, we can leverage those insights to digitally re-engage our prospects and customers and curate their experiences, all designed to get them to buy our products and services.

That's today. As for tomorrow, we need to think about the future in three phases or emerging horizons.

Horizon 1

In Horizon 1, which is underway now and will last another two to four years, AI will impact engagement at scale, vis-à-vis technology like recommendation engines in B2B marketing. The sorts of things that Amazon and Netflix do in offering suggestions such as "If you like this, you might like that" and "people who bought this also bought X" will become commonplace in B2B marketing. That's because AI suggests specific content that should appeal to the people you are trying to reach. A practical example is predictive content in emails and on websites. Content specific to an individual based on their digital persona—which you will have built in a customer database—can be delivered in real time.

Horizon 2

We are beginning to see the trappings of Horizon 2, but I expect this phase to mature in 2018 and 2019. This is where AI systems become much more adept at aiding marketers in understanding both their current audience and identifying new ones. AI will provide incredible insight into audience characteristics, attributes, and values, driving much more precision into our marketing efforts. This will have a massive impact at a practical level.

Furthermore, in Horizon 2 the marketer is going to have a broader range of AI-augmented choices. Today, there are predictive audience segmentation and lead scoring solutions, but they haven't really converged. They are hyper-specialized. In Horizon 2, you'll see those technologies start to come together. For example, an audience segmentation engine will be integrated directly into your campaign engine so that, if the preferences of your audience change, the system will be able to respond without you needing to intervene.

The potential impact of this is profound, because if I'm a B2B marketer, I may have 2,000 different digital marketing campaigns running simultaneously across social media, mobile, web, email, ads, and on and on. If the preferences of my audience change, think about all the physical work and cost associated with manually updating all those digital activities. Think about how impactful it will be to have an intelligent assistant/engine that can accomplish much of the updating work for you. Automatically.

Horizon 3

Let's move on to Horizon 3, which will be here by 2025, if not before. There are going to be end-to-end deep-learning systems that are both inferential and creative in marketing.

What I mean by inferential and creative is this: Marketing AI will make connections across multiple systems, just as humans do. If someone sees a row of apple trees, they can make an inference that it's not just a row of apple trees, but an orchard. AI will make similar connections. We will get to the point where we will be able to select a specific audience and desired outcome within our marketing automation systems and then watch as the system builds out a campaign for us. Definitely powerful, but there's a lot of code to be written between now and then. That said, this will arrive far more quickly than most marketers believe.

Imagine a pharmaceutical company producing a drug for a specific disease. The company knows the type of doctors it should market to based on their specializations, but AI allows this company to uncover other medical professionals that can also benefit from knowledge of the drug.

AI enables the pharmaceutical company to expand its marketing base but also determine the optimal time to market to them based on historical data for when prescriptions are filled for competing or complementary medications. Using information on market penetration in the pharmaceutical company's database, AI can recommend and adjust the cadence of communication with medical professionals, as well as what types of content will be most useful for them. AI then optimizes the content–from format to method of delivery–for each group of medical providers. It does this based on what channel they engage with most, what types of content they are most likely to consume, and even what format types will most appeal to their needs. By understanding what other conditions are most commonly found in patients who need a specific medication, AI can highlight new potential patient segments, empowering doctors to focus on preventative care and spot warning signs earlier.

THE MACHINE WILL MAKE THINGS MORE HUMAN

There is a marketing change already underway in the form of AI. Mathematics—more specifically, algorithms—are becoming incredibly good at understanding and, more importantly, predicting buyers' behavior and preferences. Those programs are so good, in fact, that certain functions and tasks marketers manually do today will either be radically transformed or simply just go away.

Let's take a couple of straightforward examples. Today, as a B2B marketer, I can use a range of tools. Let's pick one I like to talk about: marketing automation.

Let's say I want to use it to build a lead acquisition campaign.

As long as we are assuming, let's assume the goal of my campaign is to identify both my existing high-value customers and then acquire additional leads for new customers who share characteristics with our existing customers.

What do we need to do?

First, analyze our existing customer base to identify our most profitable customers. Most marketers today use what I would characterize as plain vanilla analytics, or basic business intelligence, to do that kind of customer analysis. However, a growing range of audience platforms, some AI-based, can complete much of this analysis for you, assuming you've fed it the right data. More importantly, not only can the AI in an audience platform tell who to target, but it can also define target audience characteristics.

Now, this may make you feel to some degree like we are operating in the Stone Age today, since we still have human beings doing this work. That's the point; it's an area that is ripe for immediate (and positive) disruption.

So, step one in our effort to build a digital marketing campaign is employing AI to identify your most profitable customers.

Step two, which is the lion's share of the work in terms of manual labor today, is the physical definition and construction of the digital marketing campaign itself (i.e., the workflow model). (As a trivial example, we send out emails every Tuesday at 3:45 p.m. to the best 500,000 customers in our database.)

Think about that for a minute. A human being has to build the campaign. In other words, someone has to select their audience, select which customers they are going after, and decide on the type of engagement channel. Is it email, is it social, is it web, is it mobile? In addition, they need to decide what type of content they are going to use to engage that person or account (based on data they've gathered about them over time).

Only after we have done all that do we click "Go." (I skipped A/B testing and a lot of other steps, lest my example drag on.)

Now multiply all that effort by the hundreds or thousands of digital marketing campaigns that sophisticated companies run every day. Think email campaigns, social campaigns, acquisition campaigns to attract new customers, education campaigns, nurture and retention campaigns to keep customers. You can see how complicated this gets. That is just the starting point.

When you start adding up all the dimensions, it becomes a very hard problem for the marketer to solve, because you have so many variables in a single equation.

But here is my contention, in two parts:

First, AI will disrupt in a positive way everything that we just talked about. It will do so by helping the marketer understand who their core audience is, who their most profitable customers are, where to find more of them, and of course, the best way to engage.

The second thing AI will do is disrupt the manual labor involved, which is very expensive, as it is quite possibly the least costly element today of operating digital marketing technologies and building things like campaigns.

AI will build and execute engagement marketing campaigns by figuring out who to target and how. But it will also be able to learn over time what a good campaign looks like and the components of a bad, or ineffective, digital marketing campaign (in a mathematical model sense). For example, an AI-based marketing automation platform will be able to determine or define a highly effective email marketing campaign targeting Millennials for a considered automotive purchase.

This is the merging of the marketer and the machine: I inform the intelligent assistant what my target audience is and what I want my desired outcome to be, and the assistant will define the campaign automatically.

It's just a matter of time, but we will get there.

The ROI on artificially intelligent marketing systems is already compelling. When we analyze our own customers' ROI in using AI-based content recommendation engines in email campaigns versus solely human-defined email campaigns, we see increases in open rates, responses, and click rates upwards of 30%. That just makes sense. The more personalized you can make digital engagement, the more likely it is someone will open the email and act on it. The trick is delivering personalized engagement at scale, something that is already a reality in the Engagement Economy.

What marketer would not want a 30% higher click-through rate from their existing campaigns? That's exactly what they can get today. Going further, within the context of engagement, what marketer wouldn't want buyers spending 30% more time on their website?

THINKING ABOUT AI CONTEXTUALLY

Today, we have autonomous vehicles. Five short years ago, would anyone have said, "There are going to be self-driving cars on public roads in 2017?" No. Unless, maybe, you are Elon Musk. Yet right now, if you look around at a stop light in Palo Alto, California, odds are you'll encounter a car with no one behind the wheel pulling up next to you. You get to enjoy a bit of a surreal moment as you contemplate the reality of the world we now live in. That is a testament to the massive leap forward that's happened in five years. I can assure you that if AI systems can safely navigate traffic in Palo Alto, they'll do just fine customizing an email. Five years from now, your Uber driver literally will be *no one*. A car will just pull up, you'll get in and go wherever your heart desires—no human involved.

Given all this, is it that much of a stretch to say, "If a vehicle is intelligent enough to drive across the country on its own, a marketing application will soon be intelligent enough to determine what content you're most likely to consume. In fact, it will start to learn on its own what your preferences and values are and start to *engage* with you in an automated fashion."

It's not a stretch. It's going to happen. Soon.

With all this said, and as exciting as it may be, I would argue that you shouldn't be thinking exclusively about life five years down the road. You should be thinking about today. I know many marketers are still at the point where they wonder if this is fact or fiction. Is it friend or foe? Is it hype or help?

Some of this may be hype today, but none of this is unachievable. And it's all coming in the foreseeable future.

THREE THINGS TO WATCH

From a machine standpoint, in a few short years there are three things that are going to massively impact engagement and marketing.

One is that chatbots will get smarter. A *lot* smarter. As in, tough-to-distinguish-from-a-human smarter. Customers today are fairly tuned in to dialoguing with customer service reps through technology like chatbots. And very soon, this will be the commonly accepted way for consumers to interact with companies online when they have questions that aren't readily answered via a help page.

Two, and probably more important, is what I would characterize as relevant content. Today, marketers waste time determining—in fact, guessing—what content they should place in front of specific human beings. Think about that in a B2B context and the complexity of today's consensus-buying scenario. You've got twenty people on a committee, and that single business value PowerPoint your account executive wrote is not going to resonate with everyone. Especially if those twenty represent a range of C-level executives, mid-level management, and some frontline employees as part of the buying group, as is usually the case.

What is happening more frequently today is that the marketer doesn't select content. The marketer creates content—at least for now. But as the machine learns and develops a digital persona, or profile of you and your likes and wants, the machine will determine in real time what content is most relevant to you. And that's the third point. We will see a significant rise in the importance of Artificial Intelligence.

To expect a human being to comprehend all the different values, wants, and needs of every individual in a single account—let alone an entire sales territory—is absurd. That's why we should embrace AI to deliver personalized experiences (again) at scale. Remember, we're talking about personalized experience at scale for millions or tens of millions or hundreds of millions or, in our new world, billions of people. It's an impossible feat for people to do without machine augmentation.

I think we've covered enough for now on AI's present and future impact on marketing. Suffice it to say that you need a plan relative to advanced engagement and marketing technologies versus just adapting what comes your way.

Now, let's get practical.

HOW DO I DECIDE WHAT TECHNOLOGY TO INVEST IN?

You can best model and determine what technology you should invest in to drive engagement, both in the short and long term, via a tool I've created to help you think through the myriad options you'll need to evaluate.

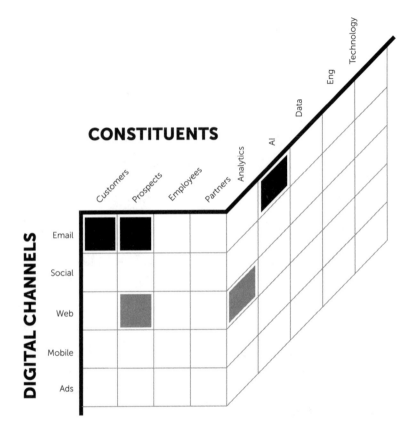

Figure 9.1 Engagement and Marketing Technology Prioritization model

In this three-dimensional graph, you'll find customers, prospects, employees, and partners as four main constituents to engage with on the x-axis. On the y-axis, you'll see all the digital channels with which to engage (i.e., email, social, web, mobile, ads, etc.). Finally, along the z-axis are the myriad technologies available today and emerging in the future that will most significantly affect your engagement strategy.

You may be concerned with how AI will impact your email lead generation and nurture campaigns for prospects and existing customers. It's worth taking the time to go through these dimensions, even add your own, and see what intersections prompt strong reaction. You might also ask, "How is data analytics going to impact my interaction with employees on the web?" Again, that's worth highlighting as shown in figure 9.1.

These three simple dimensions create literally thousands of intersections. It's not meant to drive your decisions but to help you wrap your head around a complex array of technologies, constituents, and channels—all of which impact your ability to engage. I've shared this model with Marketo customers who have literally created twenty-page technology road maps based on different intersections that interest or concern them. My goal is to give you a simple construct so that you can start building a plan.

PREPARING FOR THIS BRAVE NEW WORLD

Before we get to AI nirvana, where the robots are doing all our marketing for us, there are some basic elements that marketers need to master.

First, we need a good handle on data. The whole "garbage in, garbage out" metaphor definitely applies here. The reality is that even the world's best self-learning algorithm will come to the wrong conclusion if you feed it the wrong data. So, if you're not operating off a good data foundation based on a standardized customer and prospect database, clear definitions of accounts, etc., then AI is not going to be beneficial to you.

Second, marketers need to have a solid handle on their analytics and data science strategy. Marketers often talk about being data-driven, but data doesn't drive people. Insights and information drive people. Data is just data. If CMOs start responding to random data, then they're going to make catastrophic mistakes.

As a CMO or marketing practitioner, you need a well-defined set of control metrics that you live and die by. It's not okay in today's world to make gut decisions considering the kinds of insights we can derive from powerful analytics tools. In fact, doing anything but living by those metrics is irresponsible.

Marketers today need a data science practice within their organization. Here's something that I find intriguing: Most studies indicate that data science is a primary concern for today's CMO, yet most of them don't have any education or background in the discipline. This juxtaposition is a difficult one to deal with, but it is no excuse for lacking the practice. Start by establishing an analytics center of excellence in your marketing organization and then expanding into data science by hiring a data scientist— one with a background in sales and marketing!

SCIENCE FACT, NOT SCIENCE FICTION

For many of today's marketers, especially those who are ten or twenty years into their careers, AI was very much science fiction when they were in school. The expectation for many of us when we graduated was that AI would impact us sometime after we colonized Mars as a species (i.e., it wasn't something we had to worry about in our lifetimes).

Well, AI is here and here to stay, and it requires investment now for you to get to the front of the pack. If you look on a continuum between art and science, where is marketing currently? It's clear marketing is moving rapidly toward science, and I'd say it's reached the point of no return. And some of the creatives in marketing don't necessarily want to operate as scientists.

The reality is that the entire marketing organization needs to be data- and insight-driven. There is no way we can keep up otherwise. There is no way to succeed in the Engagement Economy without science. The best marketers agree.

"In the future, CMOs and their organizations, will need to organize around the customer and leverage data to extract insights to respond to customers in real time," said Guy Longworth, Senior Vice President and Chief Marketing Officer at Intuit. "They will do this through AI and machine learning to deliver personalized communications across all customer touchpoints. Their mission will be to continue to surprise and delight their customers. How you staff against this backdrop will determine your next generation of leadership."

Marilyn Mersereau, CMO of Plantronics, ties all this together beautifully. "I think that most marketing organizations, especially those in B2B businesses, struggle with the personalization aspect of the Engagement Economy," she says. "However, more and more are leveraging technology, such as predictive analytics, to make their marketing more contextual and relevant to their audience."

In other words, the merging of the marketer and the machine will drive engagement to new heights.

TEN

A Call to Action

What you have just read is my engagement decree.

A decree is, by definition, the pronouncement of a belief—but it is much more than that. It is the planting of a flag, the drawing of a line, the pursuit of a destiny.

Recall the seven reasons why engagement improves the return on your marketing investment:

1. You win more customers, faster.

2. You weaken your competition.

3. Customers stay with you longer.

4. You build a barrier to competition.

5. It is easier to get customers to buy more.

6. You achieve higher margins.

7. You create brand advocates.

Of course, the intention of this book is to empower *you* to engage more, and to that end you will need your need your own decree—your own personal expression of what you believe and how you see your craft evolving in a future that's arriving earlier than expected.

I invite you to begin the process of writing that decree now.

REMEMBER YOUR GOAL

As you write down your aspirations and goals, be sure to draw a distinction between brand loyalty and brand advocacy. Many marketers think they are the same thing, but they are vastly different. If you confuse the two as you set about trying to reorganize your company, you will end up building the foundation of your new organization on very shaky footing.

There's an easy way to make the distinction between loyalty and brand advocacy. Think about a company that you are loyal to because you have no choice. It could be the airline company you always try to fly. The cable company you use or maybe your CRM software.

You have accumulated hundreds of thousands of frequent flyer miles with your airline and "status," which gives you the right to board early and not pay to check a bag, so you don't want to give that up. You have to stick with your cable company because it offered you a "triple play" discount for buying your TV, phone, and Internet from them, and the price you pay for those services will rise dramatically if you cancel and go with someone else. You have a contract with your CRM provider that would be extremely expensive to break.

Yes, you are loyal to your airline, cable company, and CRM provider, but it is obligatory to some degree. You have no viable alternative.

Your goal as you start to transform your organization should be to drive beyond brand loyalty to brand advocacy.

As we've discussed, advocates are truly passionate about your brand.

Throughout the book, we have talked about why advocates are important. It is because of their influence. We are certainly in the Engagement Economy, but we are in an influencing economy as well. In the Engagement Economy, customers are engaging with other buyers as they make purchasing decisions, and they are being influenced more than ever by peers. That's why advocacy is more important today for both B2B and B2C.

To help you get started, ask yourself, "What tactics am I currently using that may be putting my organization in danger? What's being done by default inside my company today that desperately needs to be questioned? Which vanity metrics—numbers that look good but really don't move the needle—need to be eliminated?"

Remember the eight Rules of Engagement:

1. Listen and develop the discipline of really understanding what your customers say.

2. Learn to take all the data you gather from customers and potential customers and turn it into insights.

3. Act on those insights by dealing with your customers the way they want you to and when they want you to.

4. Never forget that you don't create the engagement process; your customers do.

5. Don't let anyone other than you define what your organization stands for.

6. Everyone in the company can influence the engagement process—for good or evil. Choose good.

7. Triple-check all content before it goes out. No outbound content for your customers, whether it is an email, a video, or whatever, should ever leave your company without being vetted by some type of focus group or feedback pool. In today's age of hyperreactivity, this is a requirement.

8. Never assume that what you knew to be true yesterday is true today. The world is evolving at an unprecedented accelerated pace in terms of norms, tastes, preferences, beliefs, biases, and on, and on, and on.

I believe your passion to engage like never before will grow and deepen over time, but I know the foundation will remain the same. I will always come out at the same place: I (and you) need to *engage to win*.

As you create it, don't hesitate to reach out to me on Twitter (@nstevenlucas) and let me know what you're thinking, discovering, wrestling with, and wondering.

It is clear we are on the right track. Where we go from here will require the best and most creative thinking ever applied to the art and science of marketing, so let's engage to win together!

About the Author

About Steve Lucas:
Steve is the chief executive officer at Marketo. He has a wealth of enterprise software experience, having held senior leadership positions at Microsoft, Crystal Decisions, Business Objects, Salesforce, and most recently, SAP. Steve began his career in field marketing and quickly expanded his responsibilities into a GM role. Steve holds a bachelor's degree in business from the University of Colorado and has served on the board of directors of organizations including SendGrid, TiVo, and the American Diabetes Association (ADA).

About Marketo:
Marketo, Inc., offers the only Engagement Platform that empowers marketers to create lasting relationships and grow revenue. Consistently recognized as the industry's innovation leader, Marketo is the trusted platform for thousands of CMOs thanks to its scalability, reliability, and openness. Marketo is headquartered in San Mateo, CA, with offices around the world, and serves as a strategic partner to large enterprises and fast-growing organizations across a wide variety of industries.